A WORKING RELATIONSHIP

A WORKING RELATIONSHIP
THE JOB DEVELOPMENT SPECIALIST'S GUIDE TO SUCCESSFUL PARTNERSHIPS WITH BUSINESS

Ellen S. Fabian, Ph.D.
Director of Research

Richard G. Luecking, M.Ed.
President

and

George P. Tilson, Jr., Ed.D.
Senior Vice President

TransCen, Inc.
Rockville, Maryland

·P A U L·H·
BROOKES
PUBLISHING CO

Baltimore • London • Toronto • Sydney

Paul H. Brookes Publishing Co.
P.O. Box 10624
Baltimore, Maryland 21285-0624

www.brookespublishing.com

Second printing, June 1996.

Third printing, July 2000.

Typeset by Brushwood Graphics, Inc., Baltimore, Maryland.
Manufactured in the United States of America by
The Maple Press Company, York, Pennsylvania.

Library of Congress Cataloging-in-Publication Data
Fabian, Ellen S.
    A working relationship : the job development
    specialist's guide to successful partnerships with
    business / Ellen S. Fabian, Richard G. Luecking,
    George P. Tilson, Jr.
        p.   cm.
    Includes bibliographical references and index.
    ISBN-1-55766-157-X :
    1. Handicapped—Employment—United States.
    2. Employees—Recruiting—United States.
    3. Employment agencies—United States.   I. Luecking,
    Richard G.   II. Tilson, George.   III. Title.
HD7256.U5F33   1994
331.5′9′0973—dc20   94-8029
                                                    CIP

British Library Cataloguing-in-Publication data are
available from the British Library.

CONTENTS

About the Authors vii
Acknowledgments ix
Foreword   *Richard E. Marriott* xi
Preface xiii
Introduction xv

SECTION I   Mutual Return on Investment—A Substantive Overview
             of Partnerships

 1 Job Placement and Business—A Groundwork for Change 3
 2 Effective Partnerships—How Do They Work? 17
 3 Preparing for Effective Partnerships 25
 4 Partnerships at Work 37

SECTION II   Job Development and Placement—A Practical
              Framework

 5 Principles for Restructuring the Job Search 55
 6 Knowing Each Customer 65
 7 Marketing to Prospective Employers 79
 8 Quality Service and Customer Satisfaction in Job Placement 87

SECTION III   Into the Future

 9 Business Consultation—An Emerging Role for Job
    Placement Professionals 99
10 A New Paradigm 111
Appendix   A Focus Group Study 123

Index 127

ABOUT THE AUTHORS

Ellen S. Fabian, Ph.D., is Director of Research at TransCen, Inc., and is on the faculty at the University of Maryland. Her career includes direct service positions as well as program development and evaluation in the areas of job placement and supported employment, with particular emphasis on developing programs and services that promote quality of life for people with significant disabilities. She has written extensively in professional journals on these topics.

Richard G. Luecking, M.Ed., is President of TransCen, Inc. He has held professional and administrative positions in the fields of rehabilitation, special education, and supported employment. He assisted the Marriott Foundation for People with Disabilities in developing its nationally replicated *Bridges . . . from school to work* transition project. He actively promotes partnerships through his association with numerous business, professional, and community organizations.

George P. Tilson, Jr., Ed.D., is Senior Vice President of TransCen, Inc., and is on the faculty at George Washington University. Since 1975, his career has centered on vocational preparation, employment, and independent living of people with disabilities. He has worked as a special educator, job placement specialist, program manager, and human resources consultant and trainer. His current specialization is translating theory into practice in the area of job development and placement.

The authors and their colleagues at TransCen have developed, implemented, and researched numerous innovations regarding the employment of people with disabilities. Established in 1986, TransCen is a nonprofit organization specializing in human resource issues that affect all aspects of employment for people with disabilities. TransCen has assisted more than 2,000 people with disabilities securing employment, and has consulted with and trained more than 700 public and private companies and organizations of all sizes. TransCen is the 1993 recipient of the Disabilities Awareness Network Quality Service Award from the American Society for Training and Development.

ACKNOWLEDGMENTS

In many respects, this book really began with Marriott Corporation and its people who have demonstrated over and over that the bottom line and the employment of people with disabilities are not incompatible. One of the key people in our early work with Marriott Corporation,[1] Mark Donovan, remains a valued partner in his present role as Director of the Marriott Foundation for People with Disabilities. Several of our other Marriott partners, particularly Laura Davis, Frank Nerney, and Maurice Wilson, have consistently steered us in the right direction, offering their advice, assistance, and "plain talk." We are especially indebted to Richard E. Marriott for his support of our work and for graciously agreeing to write the foreword for this book.

There are many other people who deserve acknowledgment, including Paul Wehman, without whose encouragement we would not have undertaken this effort; the charter Board of Directors of TransCen, Inc. and the Montgomery County, Maryland, government, whose collective vision included full employment for people with disabilities through collaboration between the private and public sectors; Kimberly White, who provided responsive and competent support during the development of this manuscript; many past and present TransCen staff and associates who believe deeply in their work and whose committed efforts contributed a great deal to the ideas contained in this book; and especially our many friends whose successful job searches taught us about customer service.

---

[1]In October, 1993, Marriott Corporation split into two separate companies, Marriott International, Inc. and Host Marriott Corporation. All references to Marriott or Marriott Corporation in this book refer to the company prior to the split.

FOREWORD

W hen my father opened a nine-seat root beer stand in 1927, he believed that the strength of the enterprise would always be its employees. That belief, that the success of a service business depends on the excellence of its employees, has been constant as Marriott has grown from its modest beginnings into the international business that it is today.

Along the way, Marriott has discovered that, if it is to prosper, it cannot afford to disregard any segment of the population in its quest for a strong, effective workforce. As a result, Marriott has, over the years, been a leader in the training and employment of people with disabilities. Today, over 6,000 valued members of Marriott's team are individuals with disabilities, and their integration into the company has become part of the corporate culture.

Recognizing the benefits of employing people with disabilities and further recognizing the need to share that experience with other businesses led my family to establish the Marriott Foundation for People with Disabilities in 1989. With a mission to enhance employment opportunities for young people with disabilities, the foundation developed the *Bridges . . . from school to work* program to serve two purposes: 1) to assist young people in the transition from special education to employment through the development of competitive work experiences, and 2) to help employers recognize and gain access to another important source of employees. *Bridges* was launched in 1990, and today operates successfully in five communities around the United States. The authors of this book, and TransCen, the organization they run, have been important partners in the development, piloting, and expansion of that program.

Marriott first worked with TransCen in 1987 to develop a corporate-driven initiative to hire, train, and accommodate people with disabilities in Montgomery County, Maryland. We were, and continue to be, attracted to their application of basic business principles to partnerships with business. Those principles include trust and respect as well as a mutual expectation of competent performance, accountability for results, and a reasonable return on investment. Each of these precepts is as critical to our dealings with employment agencies as to any other business relationship.

Since the days of my dad's root beer stand, a guiding principle of Marriott has been total commitment to customer service. Our reputation in the hospitality industry and our business success would not have been possible without it. In their work on behalf of people with disabilities, the authors of this book have applied this same tenet of customer service to the relationships they have with employers of every size and description. As a result, hundreds of people with disabilities have been productively employed while hundreds of businesses have successfully met human resource needs—all in all, a pretty good return on investment.

I heartily endorse TransCen, what they do, and how they do it. This book captures the key ingredients of their success. I strongly encourage human services professionals who want to build successful relationships with business to seriously consider what follows.

Richard E. Marriott
Chairman, Host Marriott Corporation
Chairman, Marriott Foundation for People with Disabilities

PREFACE

"You can observe a lot just by watching"
—Yogi Berra

Although baseball icon Yogi Berra's adages are legendary as being malapropisms, they almost always contain an important perception. In this case, what he meant—learn by watching—is exactly what became the genesis for this book. We have had occasion to spend time watching the most successful business operations at work, and we have learned from what we have seen. We have learned about customer service, mutuality in business partnerships, and excellence in human resource management. We also have learned that rehabilitation agencies, job placement professionals, and people with disabilities who are involved in creating employment opportunities have a lot to offer the business community.

Similarly, we have learned a lot by watching the manner in which employment services for people with disabilities have traditionally developed. For example, we have noticed that too many job placement professionals still rely on a "beg, place, and pray" model of job placement, whereby employer contacts look more like charitable appeals than business-to-business propositions. We have also observed that too many employment programs continue to focus only on the needs of individual jobseekers while overlooking the needs of employers. In addition, too few job placement agencies have a mission based on the premise that every individual can become a contributing member of the workforce.

Our experience in collaborating with a range of corporations, small businesses, and public employers indicates that job placement professionals must do the following in order to truly effect a change in the way job placement agencies conduct business with employers:

1. Actively address employers' concerns, fears, and misconceptions about people with disabilities. At the same time, actively encourage all people, including professionals, parents, service providers, and teachers, to recognize the talents and capabilities of people with disabilities.
2. Refocus on job development and placement as the *most* important activity within organizations representing jobseekers with disabilities. The ability to establish partnerships with employers is contingent upon valuing and rewarding the work of job placement professionals.
3. Recognize the role that job placement and other employment services have in building community. Organizations representing people with disabilities are an integral part of employment and community development. Professionals must assume both credit and responsibility for this role.
4. Operate proactively, not reactively, in the business world. Job placement professionals can't afford to wait for customers to seek them out; they must rather launch themselves into the business market because their services are indeed valuable.
5. Finally, job placement professionals must examine from the inside-out their perceptions regarding and commitment to delivering quality services. Without quality, professionals should not be in the service business.

In writing this book, we have watched how these five fundamental activities can affect the development of successful business relationships. They hint at underlying values about ourselves, our roles, and our customers. In this sense, this book is about developing value-driven partnerships that reshape the way we go about the business of opening up the workplace for people with disabilities. As one of our employer customers once said, "Over the past 5 years of watching and working with your organization, I have learned a lot about people with disabilities, about the workplace, and even about myself. It has been among the most important professional relationships in my career" (J. Brown, personal communication, April, 1993). Indeed, people can observe a lot just by watching, and they must ultimately have the commitment to act on what they observe.

INTRODUCTION

For the most part, people who gravitate toward the job placement field tend to be enthusiastic, idealistic, and dedicated. Unfortunately, they too frequently encounter significant barriers to attaining professional status. Barriers include such things as a lack of promotion potential in the direct service role, limited recognition from placement agencies, the perception of job development and placement as entry-level pursuits, limited training, and few financial rewards—a problem endemic to most human services. There are certainly job placement professionals who aspire to other roles, management, for example; but what about the experienced job placement professional who wants to continue in the direct service role? Doesn't it make sense to provide an avenue for such a person to become a senior staff member who can not only provide excellent direct service, but who can act as a mentor to staff entering the field? Ideally, this volume will help facilitate the emergence of such professionals.

What skills are actually needed by job placement professionals? The authors have spent much time over the years interacting with and working alongside personnel from many different agencies. When job placement staff at many of these agencies were recently asked to list their responsibilities, the responses numbered close to 50—50 separate and unique tasks necessary to carry out job placement goals. A close look at these responses revealed that they could be categorized according to the following: marketing, sales, public relations, vocational evaluation, public speaking, counseling, consultation, job coaching, training, and technical assistance. Indeed, job placement can be seen as encompassing all activities related to the employment of people with disabilities.

Clearly, the job placement role in an organization is a complex one comprising an immense scope of responsibility. Constantly developing new skills—or at the very least refining existing ones—is imperative in this field.

Indeed, job placement today is not the same as it was 2 decades ago. The Americans with Disabilities Act, the proliferation of disability management programs, and the creation of systems for training and supporting employees with disabilities in the workplace all suggest dramatic developments in job placement practices. These developments call for dynamic new partnerships—partnerships based on mutuality and the sharing of power, decision making, and responsibilities for outcomes. They have at their core the principle that attention to customer service will ultimately result in customer satisfaction, and they thus promise a mutual return on investment.

To all of TransCen's customers

A Working Relationship

MUTUAL RETURN ON INVESTMENT— A SUBSTANTIVE OVERVIEW OF PARTNERSHIPS

Chapter 1

JOB PLACEMENT AND BUSINESS— A GROUNDWORK FOR CHANGE

In 1972, one of the authors of this book got his first job as a vocational rehabilitation counselor in a small town in southern Illinois. His job was to place people with disabilities into competitive employment. Antidiscrimination legislation protecting individuals with disabilities had not been passed and training and employment innovations such as supported employment and many assistive technology devices did not yet exist. The only mass media attention to people with disabilities consisted of charitable telethons and "hire the handicapped" campaigns. In addition to all of this, the general unemployment rate in southern Illinois was 17%.

Against this background, how did this neophyte vocational rehabilitation counselor find jobs for the people he represented? He begged employers for jobs, he placed people in available jobs, and he prayed that they would succeed.

Since 1972, legislative and social changes have precipitated an end to this "beg, place, and pray" scenario. The Rehabilitation Act of 1973, PL 93-112, was the first federal legislation prohibiting employment discrimination against people with disabilities. In 1990, this legislation was superseded by the Americans with Disabilities Act, PL 101-336, hailed as landmark antidiscrimination legislation on a par with the 1964 Civil Rights Act. Federal initiatives such as supported employment and transition from school-to-work programs have also contributed to creating a climate wherein there has been significant change in the way that the public, job placement professionals, and employers view employment of people with disabilities. Indeed, in this last decade of the 20th century, people with disabilities, advocates, and job placement professionals are seeing the next century as one of tremendous opportunity in the workplace. This opportunity is being created by new legislation, new business trends, and changes in the workplace.

However, there are also indications that job placement programs and other rehabilitation agencies are overlooking these opportunities. Like businesses, these agencies have had to grapple with the economic hardships and changes in the labor pool
that occurred in the late 1980s and 1990s.

From the standpoint of social services, as more people are in need, publicly
funded programs suffer as the tax base erodes and business battles hard times
(Weaver, 1991). Specifically regarding jobseekers with disabilities, fewer jobs are available and the programs that assist them are experiencing funding cutbacks. Ironically,
just when job placement services are needed most, they are least available.

The story of one job placement professional is illustrative. Responding to a period
of economic recession, the vocational director of a large job placement agency wrote to
warn its clients that fewer jobs would be available to them. The letter discussed job
competition and how clients were competing for the same jobs that people without
disabilities wanted. Although the director and staff at the agency were doing their
best, their approach precluded recognizing the opportunities often hidden in difficult times.

To compete successfully in the changing workplace of the 21st century, business
must pay attention to changing labor demographics, diversity in the workplace, and
human resource management issues. Efforts to attract, train, and accommodate a diverse labor force are driving businesses to redesign their workplaces. Herein lies the
job placement professional's opportunity: rather than giving in to a competitive marketplace and the notion that employers have other constituent groups who are seeking
the same quality jobs as are people with disabilities, job placement and other human
services agencies can offer employers services that were previously unavailable. Job
placement professionals, indeed, can respond directly to business's needs; after all,
analyzing, redesigning, accommodating, and integrating are the benchmarks of their
work. Previous objectives that focus on trying to increase internal resources—money,
time, and staff—are being replaced by goals measured by specific outcomes. To share
power, resources, and responsibility for outcomes requires attention to external measures of success such as customer satisfaction. This is, in fact, one of the most important lessons that job placement agencies can learn from business.

The "beg, place, and pray" scenario is being replaced with a new ethic of quality
services and customer satisfaction that characterizes job placement agencies as they
strive to re-invent themselves. There are demographic, social, and political trends that
can succeed in assisting these agencies in change. This chapter describes these trends
as they affect business and employment opportunities for people with disabilities
through the next century.

TODAY'S WORKFORCE

As businesses struggle for competitive and organizational success, they will need to
plan for, rather than react to, a changing workforce. Profitability will be affected by
how skillfully companies manage employees. Shifts in American demographics (e.g.,
growing diversity, the new skills required for the modern workplace, and the new
demands of employees) are forcing changes in workplace cultures and services.

The Multicultural Marketplace and Workplace

The multicultural society reflected in the expanding multicultural workforce presents
the need for change in American industry, government, and educational institutions

(Loden & Rosener, 1991). Successful competition in the future requires recognizing, respecting, and capitalizing on this diversity. Consider the following:

- During the 1990s, people of color, Caucasian women, and immigrants will account for 85% of the net growth in the United States labor force (Johnston & Packer, 1987).
- In 1980, women made up 43% of the total workforce. By the year 2000, they will account for more than 47% of the total workforce, and 61% of all American women will be employed (Johnston & Packer, 1987).
- By the end of the 1990s, African Americans will make up 12% of the total labor force, Hispanics 10%, and Asians 4% (Kiplinger & Kiplinger, 1989).
- The American workforce will continue to mature, with those in the 35–54 age group increasing by more than 25 million—from 34% of the workforce in 1985 to 51% by the year 2000. At the same time, those in the 16–34 age group will decline by almost 2 million, or 8% (Johnston & Packer, 1987).
- Among the top 25 urban markets throughout the United States, people of color now make up the majority population in 16 (Donnelly Marketing Information Services, 1988).

For United States business, valuing diversity is as much a bottom-line issue as it is a social, moral, and legal one.

New Supports in the Workplace

Changes in demographics and worker preparation, as well as environmental concerns—particularly the rising costs of commuting to work—and the strong correlation between quality of work life and quality of life, mean that employers are trying to bridge the gap between home and work life. The implications for business—job placement partnerships are numerous: forging creative new ways of performing jobs, incorporating flexibility in employees' work lives, and restructuring job demands to meet individual needs.

Bridging the gap between home and work life involves more than innovations in the workplace, however. An array of social support services are becoming more frequently available within corporate environments. In the past, on-site support services were generally limited to work-relevant supports such as mentoring, career development, and education and training. The 1980s and 1990s have seen expansion of these services to address more personal concerns (e.g., health and mental health) as well as personal development (e.g., literacy training and English as a second language programs). Many of these employee support services grew out of human resource management philosophies predicated on the notion that better management practices result in better productivity.

This fundamental shift in managing human resources precipitated the initiation of a variety of employee support services in the workplace. Below is a list of a few of these services:

- *Flex time*—The explosion in the number of women in the workplace created the need for this widely practiced accommodation. The need for employees to arrange their work schedules around school and childcare arrangements necessitated flexible start and end times of the business day.
- *Dependent on-site care*—Single parents, two career families, and the "sandwich generation" (i.e., people who care for their parents as well as their children) forced employers to consider this option as a solution to absenteeism and decreased productivity.

- *Job sharing*—Splitting a job between two part-time employees can be an attractive option to applicants whose circumstances prohibit full-time work (e.g., retirees, homemakers, and students). In fact, organizations frequently find that the total performance of two part-time employees exceeds that which is ordinarily expected from one full-time employee.
- *Telecommunication*—Working at home through the use of a computer and word processing equipment linked to a company's office will likely involve as many as 15 million workers in the United States by the year 2000.
- *Other work scheduling patterns*—Compressed work weeks, permanent part-time work, and liberalized use of compensatory time for overtime are other examples of how companies are responding to workforce needs.
- *Job redesign, enrichment, and restructuring*—All of these approaches are used by companies to increase workers' motivation, productivity, and job satisfaction.

Enhancing skill and task variety has been used by the most effective managers for as long as there has been work, but it is evident that companies are making what just a few years ago would have been considered extraordinary efforts to attract, train, accommodate, and retain workers. Indeed, businesses are investing in the workforce. These efforts are based on competition for employees and the need to maintain a high level of productivity in increasingly competitive markets (Fabian & Luecking, 1991).

Economic need, competition, and the desire for profits have important implications for partnerships between business and job placement. Indeed, job placement can offer important technical assistance to business as it looks to redirect training resources to both entry-level and on-line workers. Business can use job placement's expertise in job analysis, training, accommodation, positive behavior management, and assistive technology. Alternatively, job placement can certainly benefit from business's knowledge regarding efficiency, economics, negotiation, motivation, and customer service.

The Implications for People with Disabilities

A recent U.S. Department of Labor study quoted the EEO manager of IBM: "Disabled persons are a great untapped resource for American business" (Hudson Institute, 1988, p. vii). Examples of employers reaching out to workers with disabilities and workers who come from different cultural groups to meet labor shortages are becoming more commonplace. The changes in U.S. demographics discussed above (particularly the declining number of young workers, which is expected to hit its nadir by the year 2000) offer new avenues for people with disabilities entering the labor market.

Other labor market trends, however, may affect opportunity for workers with disabilities. Requirements for increasingly sophisticated skills in an advancing technological age have been documented (Boyett & Conn, 1991). Unfortunately, current surveys regarding people with disabilities indicate that the majority have not received the necessary education and training to serve effectively in the job market. Indeed, 40% of people with disabilities do not finish high school, compared to 15% of people without disabilities (Louis Harris & Associates, 1986). "The quality of training is going to make a big difference in the opportunities that will become available to disabled individuals. Right now, training is often out-of-date, geared toward jobs that do not exist or are on their way out" (Hudson Institute, 1988, p. 11). If people with disabilities aren't learning the skills required to succeed in this new workplace, are they destined to be underemployed, relegated to entry-level jobs with no hope of future advancement? On the surface, it would seem so.

In 1971, 58% of the population of people with disabilities were unemployed; 66% were estimated to be unemployed by 1990. Of men with disabilities who are working, only 17% hold full-time, year-round jobs, compared to 63% of their counterparts without disabilities. Furthermore, these men earn 63% of what workers without disabilities earn (Oi, 1991). People with disabilities who are working have a median family income of $6,000, compared to $13,000 for their counterparts who do not have disabilities. Of families that have a member with a disability, 25% have incomes below poverty levels (Kraus & Stoddard, 1989).

The picture grows worse when one examines labor force participation for women and members of minority ethnic groups who have disabilities. For these groups, the chance of being competitively employed is even slimmer. For example, the rate of employment for African Americans with disabilities is less than 25% (Kraus & Stoddard, 1989). Underscoring these dismal figures is the explosion in expenditures in Social Security income benefit programs for unemployed people with disabilities: from $5 billion in the early 1970s to $30 billion in 1990 (U.S. Social Security Administration, 1993).

These data are not necessarily indicative of the inability of people with disabilities. However, they are consistent with the social and legal barriers that have impeded their entry into the workplace. Unfortunately, people with disabilities are an untapped resource for business. Furthermore, job placement agencies are a resource for business in terms of technical assistance, workplace accommodations, and meeting the challenge of diversity. An historical look at where we have been in the field will establish the context for exploring business partnerships in this regard.

ENABLING LEGISLATION

Enabling legislation provided the groundwork to change this bleak picture for prospective employees with disabilities. In 1973, the first federal legislation prohibiting employment discrimination against people with disabilities was enacted. PL 93-112, the Rehabilitation Act of 1973, forbade discrimination on the basis of "handicapping conditions" in employment and delivery of federally funded services. Other landmark legislation soon followed. The Education for All Handicapped Children Act of 1975, PL 94-142, granted "free, appropriate, public education" to all children regardless of disability. PL 95-602, the Developmental Disabilities Assistance and Bill of Rights Act, followed in 1978. At the same time came the first set of amendments to the Rehabilitation Act of 1973 (PL 93-112), which employed a more functional approach to identifying disability among its many provisions. Further amendments in 1986 (PL 99-506) established the concept of supported employment. Then, in 1990, the legislation that has been hailed as the most significant antidiscrimination legislation since the Civil Rights Act of 1964 was passed: the Americans with Disabilities Act (ADA), PL 101-336.

The ADA prohibits discrimination against people with disabilities in public and private sector labor markets and provides individual remedies for people who have been discriminated against. The ADA goes beyond prohibiting discrimination, as it also requires employers to provide reasonable accommodation that will allow qualified people with disabilities to perform essential job functions. Policy analysts have described the ADA as being both a nondiscrimination and an affirmative action law (Weaver, 1991). Senator Tom Harkin, co-sponsor of the ADA in the Senate, calls it the "emancipation proclamation" for people with disabilities (McCrone, 1990).

Obstacles

Further reflection on the analogy between the ADA and the Civil Rights Act suggests, however, that the ADA alone will not improve employment for people with disabilities. A 1988 U.S. Department of Labor study observed that, "despite the combined impact of equal opportunity laws, the growing shortage of labor, and an increasing share of minorities in the labor force, many minority individuals remain outside the economic mainstream" (Hudson Institute, 1988, p. 9). In fact, labor statistics cited in that study indicated that some minority populations, particularly young African American males, saw declines in labor force participation over the 20-year period from 1965 to 1984. Part of the problem may be traced to increased opportunities for those from higher income families and decreased opportunities for those from lower income backgrounds. The ADA and citizens working to implement it face several ongoing, difficult issues. Inconsistent definitions of disability, a historically unreceptive employer base, a beleaguered Social Security system, and a Vocational Rehabilitation system entrenched in outmoded practices hinder attainment of the promise of the ADA.

Disability Undefined

The difficulty in defining disability presents a dilemma that potentially influences hiring. Under other equal protection legislation, for example, it is relatively easy to classify people by gender, race, or age. However, the categorization or determination of what constitutes disability differs among various federal programs. Indeed, there are 43 different federal definitions of disability (Kemp, 1991). For instance, the definition of disability for Social Security Disability Insurance (SSDI) benefits is based on a clinical concept of impairment, whereby certain medical eligibility standards that make an individual unable to "engage in any substantial gainful activity" must be met (U.S. Social Security Administration, 1993, p. 64). For the ADA, the definition of disability is necessarily much broader, stipulating that coverage under the act is extended to "persons with physical or mental impairments that substantially limit one or more of the major life activities, people with a history of such impairment, and people regarded as having such an impairment."

In a fascinating exploration of the evolution of the "disability category," Stone (1984) points out that, not only is the category variously defined, but it also appears to be continuously expanding. For example, federal legislation now includes people with alcoholism, people with a variety of occupationally caused impairments such as black-lung disease, and people experiencing work-related stress. The ADA similarly covers people who use wheelchairs, people who are legally blind, people who are recovering from drug and alcohol abuse, people who are human immunodeficiency virus (HIV) positive, and people who have a host of other physical and mental impairments. Although other antidiscrimination legislation designed to protect classes of people defined by race or age makes it relatively easy to decide if individuals meet the criteria for belonging to one of those classes, the vastness and imprecision of the disability category make some determinations difficult, particularly for those people with "hidden" disabilities who may not wish to disclose their disability to potential employers.

BUSINESS GROWTH TRENDS

Expectations that most new growth is expected to be in small business may also significantly affect the participation of people with disabilities in the labor force. Business growth trends indicate that two-thirds of the growth in U.S. companies over the past decade has been in those with fewer than 25 employees (U.S. Department of Commerce, 1992). Offsetting this, however, are two significant factors.

First, the Hudson Institute (1988) cited the fact that most successful examples of the corporate world aiding underrepresented workers come from corporate giants such as Marriott, IBM, and McDonald's. Furthermore, a survey conducted by Louis Harris and Associates (1987) found that only 16% of companies employing 10–49 workers had hired someone with a disability in a 1-year period, compared to 52% of companies of 10,000 or more employees. Furthermore, the same study showed that companies employing at least 10,000 people are two to nine times more likely to have a hiring policy for people with disabilities than are companies with less than 1,000 employees. Can small entrepreneurial businesses with few employees and fewer resources be expected to follow this example?

Second, the provisions of the ADA apply only to businesses with more than 15 employees. In small communities, rural areas, inner cities, and enterprise zones, most new businesses are small and entrepreneurial (U.S. Department of Commerce, 1992). Although the impact of the growth of small businesses may not seem important, the issue of working with employers who are not "covered entities" according to the provisions of the ADA is an issue facing all job placement agencies.

A Social Security System in Crisis

One of the most frequently cited barriers to people with disabilities achieving full participation in the competitive labor market is the federal Social Security program (Berkowitz, 1987; Weaver, 1991). Through the 1980s, politicians decried the rapid expansion of the Social Security benefits program. Despite President Ronald Reagan's efforts to eliminate malingerers and welfare cheaters from disability roles, many of those "purged" retained their benefits upon appeal, and the Social Security benefits program thus continued to grow; by 1991, $16 billion was spent on cash benefits for people with disabilities (U.S. Social Security Administration, 1993). Proponents of this type of federal funding argue that these benefits are part of a cost–benefit ratio that makes taxpayers out of tax beneficiaries. This cost–benefit argument would be a compelling one if it didn't miss the monumental social paradox in the Social Security system: the issue is not who becomes the recipient of federal aid, but that the system makes disability both a "privilege" and a stigma.

On the one hand, to be eligible for cash benefits from the government, individuals with disabilities must "prove" their "total incapacity" to work by satisfying specific criteria (i.e., they must adopt what sociologists call the disabled role [Parsons, 1958]). On the other hand, entry into the workforce hinges on the ability to prove to employers that individuals with disabilities do have the capacity to perform. When the Social Security Administration responded to pressure from the U.S. Congress to put into place "work incentives" under Section 1619 of the Employment Opportunities for Disabled Americans Act (PL 99-643), it was attempting to address more obvious barriers in the system. In the past, if people with disabilities got jobs, they lost the medical benefits associated with receipt of Social Security assistance. Simple measures such as reinstating medical benefits, however, ignore the more pervasive disincentives built into the current Social Security system. Like those disincentives built into welfare programs in general, these barriers to change are even more implacable and require more expansive solutions. The defining of disability as inability underscores the problem. People in job placement have long known that, once people are categorized as "disabled," there exists the danger of their being socialized into that role (Parsons, 1958). Indeed, the longer people do not work, the less likely they are to return to work (Lam, Bose, & Geist, 1989).

The three most popular remedies to the current Social Security dilemma— 1) purging the rolls, 2) enacting work incentives, and 3) strengthening vocational rehabilitation (Stone, 1984)—all assume that the problem resides with the recipient of the benefits rather than with the system by which those benefits are allocated. As long as there is a system imposing categorization based on standards such as "total incapacity" and "impairment," the work of job placement professionals will remain challenging. Berkowitz (1987) predicts that Social Security's entitlement guidelines for people with disabilities will not change. The issue that job placement professionals are facing, therefore, is how to develop innovative programs despite this barrier.

The State Vocational Rehabilitation Program

The Vocational Rehabilitation program also unintentionally creates barriers to employment for people with disabilities. Created in 1920 with enabling legislation (PL 66-236), its purpose was to provide for the vocational rehabilitation of "persons disabled in industry or in any legitimate occupation." Though small through its first 30 years of existence, this federal program's expenditures and popularity exploded during the 1950s and 1960s. Indeed, the federal budget for Vocational Rehabilitation services has grown enormously over its more than 50-year history. It not only provides most of the funding in each state for direct Vocational Rehabilitation services for people with disabilities, but it also supports special demonstrations, supported employment programs, research, and professional training of job placement personnel through a variety of discretionary grant programs.

Expansion of this Vocational Rehabilitation program was due in large measure to its success. During what some call the golden years of rehabilitation—the late 1960s and early 1970s—the rehabilitation rate in the federal program (i.e., the number of successful job closures in comparison to the number of people referred) was 77% (U.S. Department of Commerce, 1990). Therefore, it was easy to persuade Congress of the effectiveness of a program that accounted for its success by such a measure. This measure could be used as part of the cost–benefit ratio in support of Vocational Rehabilitation services. In the 1970s, for example, RSA administrators could say that this federal program was one of the few that paid itself back to the taxpayers: for every dollar spent, a successful rehabilitant returned at least 10 times that to the economy (Berkowitz, 1987).

During the next decade, however, circumstances began to change. The Rehabilitation Act of 1973, PL 93-112, mandated that the Vocational Rehabilitation program prioritize services for people with "severe" disabilities. It was enacted directly in response to charges by disability advocates that the system was serving those who needed it least, namely, individuals who might have gotten jobs without assistance. Not surprisingly, from a high of 324,000 rehabilitants in 1975, the number of successful rehabilitants slipped to 218,000 in 1988 (U.S. Department of Commerce, 1990).

Disenchantment grew as disability advocates further charged that the program fostered dependency rather than empowered independence. Rehabilitation professionals, commented one advocate who was disabled,

> reduce our ability to function independently because they give you the impression that they're the ones who know what's good for you. They reduce your belief that you can solve your own problems. They therefore reduce your motivation to get things sorted out in your own life. So then they produce somebody who'll come and deal with your lack of motivation." (Sutherland, 1981, p. 23)

Other factors as well contributed to the difficulties experienced by the public Vocational Rehabilitation program. These included an expanding base of eligible individuals to serve, lengthy determinations of eligibility resulting in long waits for services, and conflicts in the roles of counselors, who often preferred counseling and case management to job placement.

In addition to these issues within the Vocational Rehabilitation program, the activists' movement among people with disabilities, which was buttressed by the passage of the ADA, focused on environmental barriers as opposed to functional deficits as explanations for problems in gaining access to employment. Disability thus became a civil rights issue in that it is not individual limitations but unequal access—to employment, to education, to transportation, to programs, and to buildings—that hinders independence (Hahn, 1985).

Internally Focused Goals of Public Service Organizations

Despite the obstacles in the public Vocational Rehabilitation program, rehabilitation counselors and job placement professionals are looking for ways to develop innovative programs and services to address those obstacles. However, regardless of their good intentions, it is extremely difficult for public service organizations to innovate for change. This includes not only the Vocational Rehabilitation program, but also the nonprofit service agencies funded by it to provide job placement services.

Public service organizations tend to base success on getting larger budgets rather than on achieving better results (Albin, 1992; Drucker, 1985). This criterion for success tends to promote the use of internal performance standards rather than external benchmarks such as customer satisfaction to evaluate a program. Indeed, the success of a program is often determined by the number of job placements made rather than by the satisfaction rate of consumers and employers.

In addition, public service organizations often have a myriad of constituencies, each with its own needs and demands. Rehabilitation agencies, for example, must satisfy consumers with disabilities, a variety of categorical funding agencies (such as state administrations for developmental disabilities and state vocational rehabilitation programs), community members, families, and employers. The confusion that arises in determining how to respond to the conflicting demands of these groups often compromises agencies' ability to innovate.

Perhaps most important, public service organizations are inclined to maximize rather than optimize their output. They set ambitious goals—finding jobs for all people with disabilities—and then seek larger dollar allocations when they fail to attain those goals. As more money is demanded in order to try to meet unrealistic goals, the result is that less is done for many by trying to do everything for all.

In sum, a vastly changing set of environmental circumstances and external pressures are shaping fundamental changes in both the private and public sectors. American businesses have experienced a significant downturn over the past few decades.

Similarly, in the public sector, declining resources are forcing social programs to downsize. Unfortunately, both businesses and human services agencies have at times demonstrated a lack of adaptation, innovation, and flexibility.

PARTNERSHIPS BASED ON MUTUALITY

Earlier in this chapter, we described partnerships as being based on mutuality in terms of sharing power, resources, and responsibility for outcomes. In order for partnerships between business and job placement agencies to achieve this mutuality, it is necessary to understand the values and beliefs that drive them. These values and beliefs form the basis for organizational cultures.

Organizational Culture

Culture may be defined as those attitudes and beliefs that guide actions. It consists of sets of implicit and explicit principles that provide a framework for individual beliefs and behaviors. Organizations, like people, have cultures. Like individual cultures, organizational cultures vary widely. Corporate cultures, for instance, not only influence the way the corporation does business, but also the ways in which it treats and views employees; values diversity; and commits to new realities like a pluralistic workforce, retrenched economics, and the corporate community (Sue, 1991).

Corporate cultures are complex. They can be exclusionary or monocultural with little tolerance for individual differences or group diversity; or they may be assimilation-oriented—accepting diverse individuals but expecting those individuals to conform or adjust to cultural standards that guide behaviors, attitudes, and beliefs. In these cases, not assimilating—or not being able to assimilate—can lead to frustration for both employees and employers.

Service Organization Cultures

Service organizations have cultures as well. These cultures are generally guided by mission statements that outline particular goals of individual agencies, and comprise the perceptions and beliefs of respective employees. The cultures of service organizations are as deeply entrenched as those of business, and are often as difficult to change (Albin, 1992).

It is not surprising that job placement agencies and business have cultural values resulting from separate and distinct assumptions. Indeed, the values and ethics of business may not be shared by job placement professionals, even when they understand that profits drive businesses and, more importantly, that profits provide fuel for change.

Over the past several years, research on cultural differences has provided considerable support for the notion that operating from different cultural assumptions affects communication, planning, and problem solving, at least in individual relationships (Carter, 1991; Pedersen, 1988). It is not difficult to extrapolate from these findings that the different sets of cultural guidelines from which businesses and job placement agencies operate may become obstacles to effective partnering. It is important for job placement personnel and employees with disabilities to understand that cultural values are pervasive; they affect not only workplace practices, but initial recruitment, retention, and promotion activities as well.

Culture and the Value of Inclusion

As important as understanding the differences between the respective cultures of job placement and business is understanding the pervasive nature of corporate culture in general. Indeed, it affects not only an individual's integration into a work environment, but initial recruitment, retention, and promotion as well (Sue, 1991). At each of these three levels—initial recruitment, retention, and promotion—myths regarding people with disabilities or the exclusionary nature of corporate cultures function as barriers to partnerships.

Most job placement literature focusing on organizational culture has implicitly endorsed the value of assimilation—trying to assist employees in fitting into environments that may not understand or value differences. Assimilation is not necessarily negative; it may, in fact, be the strategy of choice for some employees with disabilities who are moving into the business world. However, if we look at the poor employment record for people with disabilities in terms of recruitment, retention, and promotion—particularly in relation to the anticipated increase in ethnic and cultural minority representation by the year 2000—then job placement personnel must realize that strategies for assimilation will become increasingly irrelevant in the 21st century workplace (Hudson Institute, 1988). Instead, business partnerships must be based on mutual benefits and the value of inclusion.

CONCLUSION

Boyett and Conn (1991) describe the company of the future as being "flatter, leaner, and more aggressive" (p. 2) than the company of today. In order to succeed, these flatter, leaner companies will place renewed emphasis on enhancing the work experience—making work more meaningful for employees by stressing inclusion and accountability in decision making and responsibility for outcomes. Thus, employees in the future can expect both to share more power and responsibility in decision making and to be held responsible for outcomes.

Boyett and Conn (1991) further state that the workplace in the year 2000 will be characterized by flexibility, new demands for quality, and team (rather than individual) performance and reward structures. Diversity, accommodation to individual needs, and technological advances that enable creative job structuring may also be added to this list. That is, the workplace of the future will not only demand more of its employees, but will also encourage partnerships by creating teams and workgroups rather than relying on vertical management structures.

In view of the history of services for people with disabilities as well as current business trends, new responses are clearly needed. Partnerships that are based on appeals to corporate good will and charity will no longer work, and relying solely on legislation to get the job done has never worked. Although the passage of the ADA and changes in business operation and American demographics represent opportunities in the job market, they are not in and of themselves innovations, but rather sources that will catalyze change. That is, they are opportunities of which to take advantage in forming new partnerships with businesses. Like United States business, United States job placement and development needs to "empower people to reach for a future different from the past" (Kanter, 1983, p. 34).

This is a realistic vision for the future, but it won't happen unless job placement personnel and employees with disabilities become agents of change and innovation.

The assumptions and strategies that have shaped job placement personnel throughout the past 50 or so years in terms of developing effective partnerships have been ineffective. Obviously, then, they will not carry us successfully into the 21st century. Problems will not disappear with the passage of new legislation or the awakening of more enlightened attitudes. Exploiting opportunities by forging new partnerships is truly the only alternative.

It can no longer be business as usual. The succeeding chapters present practical strategies that enable dynamic partnerships between business and rehabilitation and job placement agencies to develop. These new partnerships call for relationships based on business principles; they affirm the fact that job placement professionals are and will continue to be valuable technical advisors to employers as they work to respond to workforce challenges through the next century.

REFERENCES

Albin, J. (1992). *Quality improvement in employment and other human services: Managing for quality through change.* Baltimore: Paul H. Brookes Publishing Co.

Americans with Disabilities Act of 1990 (ADA), PL 101-336. (July 26, 1990). Title 42, U.S.C. 12101 et seq: *U.S. Statutes at Large, 104,* 327–378.

Berkowitz, E.D. (1987). *Disabled policy: America's programs for the handicapped.* London: Cambridge University Press.

Boyett, J.H., & Conn, H.P. (1991). *Workplace 2000: The revolution reshaping American business.* New York: Plume.

Carter, R.T. (1991). Cultural values: A review of empirical research and implications for counseling. *Journal of Counseling and Development, 70,* 164–173.

Civil Rights Act of 1964, PL 88-352. (July 2, 1964). Title 42, U.S.C. 1971 et seq: *U.S. Statutes at Large, 78,* 241–286.

Developmental Disabilities Assistance and Bill of Rights Act of 1975, PL 94-103. (October 4, 1975). Title 42, U.S.C. 6000 et seq: *U.S. Statutes at Large, 89,* 486–507.

Developmental Disabilities Assistance and Bill of Rights Act of 1978, PL 95-602. (November 6, 1978). Title 5, U.S.C. 6000 et seq: *U.S. Statutes at Large, 92,* 3003–3004.

Donnelly Marketing Information Services. (1988). *D & B donnelly demographics.* Stamford, CT: Author.

Drucker, P.F. (1985). *Innovation and entrepreneurship.* New York: Harper & Rowe.

Education for All Handicapped Children Act of 1975, PL 94-142. (August 23, 1977). Title 20, U.S.C. 1401 et seq: *U.S. Statutes at Large, 89,* 773–796.

Employment Opportunities for Disabled Americans Act, PL 99-643. (November 10, 1986). Title 42, U.S.C. 1305 et seq: *U.S. Statutes at Large, 100,* 3574–3577.

Fabian, E.S., & Luecking, R.G. (1991). Doing it the company way: Using internal company supports in the workplace. *Journal of Applied Rehabilitation Counseling, 22,* 22–26.

Hahn, H.L. (1985). Toward a politics of disability: Definitions, disciplines, and policies. *The Social Science Journal, 22,* 87–105.

Hudson Institute. (1988). *Opportunity 2000: Creative affirmative action strategies for a changing workforce* (Contract No. 99-6-3370-75-002-02). Washington, DC: U.S. Government Printing Office.

Johnston, W., & Packer, A. (1987). *Workforce 2000: Work and workers for the twenty-first century.* Indianapolis: Hudson Institute.

Kanter, R.M. (1983). *The change masters.* New York: Simon & Schuster.

Kemp, E.J. (1991). Disability in our society. In C.L. Weaver (Ed.), *Disability and work* (pp. 56–58). Washington, DC: American Enterprise Institute.

Kiplinger, A., & Kiplinger, K. (1989). *America in the global '90s.* Washington, DC: Kiplinger Books.

Kraus, L.E., & Stoddard, S. (1989). *Chartbook on disability in the United States* (Contract No. HN 88011001). Washington, DC: U.S. Government Printing Office.

Lam, C.S., Bose, J.L., & Geist, G.O. (1989). Employment outcome of private rehabilitation clients. *Rehabilitation Counseling Bulletin, 32,* 300–311.

Loden, M., & Rosener, J. (1991). *Workforce America!: Managing employee diversity as a vital resource.* Homewood, IL: Business One Irwin.

Louis Harris & Associates, Inc. (1986). *The ICD survey of disabled Americans: Bringing disabled Americans into the mainstream.* New York: International Center for the Disabled.

Louis Harris & Associates, Inc. (1987). *The ICD survey II: Employing disabled Americans.* New York: International Center for the Disabled.

McCrone, W.P. (1990). Senator Tom Harkin: Reflections on disability policy. *Journal of Rehabilitation, 56,* 9.

Oi, W.Y. (1991). Disability and a workforce–welfare dilemma. In C.L. Weaver (Ed.), *Disability and work* (pp. 31–45). Washington, DC: American Enterprise Institute.

Parsons, T. (1958). Definitions of health and illness in light of American values and social structure. In E.G. Jasco (Ed.), *Patients, physicians and health* (pp. 165–187). Glencoe, IL: Free Press.

Pedersen, P. (1988). *A handbook for developing multicultural awareness.* Alexandria, VA: American Association for Counseling and Development.

Rehabilitation Act of 1973, PL 93-112. (September 26, 1973). Title 29, U.S.C. 701 et seq: *U.S. Statutes at Large, 87,* 355–394.

Rehabilitation Act Amendments of 1986, PL 99-506. (October 21, 1986). Title 29, U.S.C. 701 et seq: *U.S. Statutes at Large, 100,* 1807–1846.

Stone, D.A. (1984). *The disabled state.* Cambridge, MA: MIT Press.

Sue, D.W. (1991). A model for cultural diversity training. *Journal of Counseling and Development, 70,* 99–105.

Sutherland, A.T. (1981). *Disabled we stand.* Bloomington, IN: Indiana University Press.

U.S. Department of Commerce. (1990). *Statistical abstracts of the United States, 1990.* Washington, DC: U.S. Government Printing Office.

U.S. Department of Commerce. (1992). *Statistical abstracts of the United States, 1992.* U.S. Government Printing Office.

U.S. Social Security Administration. (1993). *Social Security bulletin.* Washington, DC: U.S. Government Printing Office.

Vocational Rehabilitation of Persons Disabled in Industry, PL 66-236, 41 Stat 735 (1919–1921).

Weaver, C.L. (Ed.). (1991). *Disability and work.* Washington, DC: American Enterprise Institute.

Chapter 2

EFFECTIVE PARTNERSHIPS— HOW DO THEY WORK?

One way to examine the efficacy and endurance of the partnerships described in Chapter 1 is to compare them to effective partnerships whose characteristics have been identified through both experience with business and interviews with employers in focus groups as well as in other settings.

BUILDING EFFECTIVE PARTNERSHIPS

There are five key characteristics that are fundamental to the development of effective partnerships between job placement agencies and businesses. Each of these is reviewed below.

Trust

Satisfactory partnerships are built on trust. In order to enter into a relationship with either a jobseeker or an employer, it is necessary to build a foundation of mutual understanding in which the key is trust. Trust is established by delivering services as promised. At the most fundamental level, it is built upon an expectation regarding a partner's ability to deliver quality services. This perception is often based on the individual relationships of job placement professionals with employers. For example, in a focus group study conducted with employers described in the appendix, the group was asked to identify those characteristics of job placement professionals that are essential to a successful relationship. Key among the characteristics identified were knowledge and understanding. When asked the same question, job placement personnel responded similarly, identifying openness and honesty as key in building relationships with employers. Indeed, mutual trust is the underlying indicator in predicting successful outcomes for employer relationships.

Goals and Objectives that Benefit Everyone Involved

Partnerships based on good will rather than good service are generally ineffective. Regardless, charity was once believed to be the major motivating factor governing businesses' decisions to work with job placement agencies or to hire jobseekers with disabilities. Little attention was given to how each partner benefited from the relationship, and job placement agencies were not viewed as credible business partners. These one-sided partnerships—those wherein employers were believed to shoulder all of the risk—were not modeled after existing business partnerships. Indeed, good partnerships require mutual investment in order to achieve mutually satisfying outcomes.

Long-Term Relationships

The existing service delivery system continues to be based on the "beg, place, and pray" model of job development. That is, job placement personnel provide quick job placements and hope that they last a requisite 60 days in order to be counted as successful. However, this type of quick in and out service is not likely to sustain lasting partnerships. Worse, individual job failures hurt the reputations of job placement agencies because initial trust is never really established.

When a relationship is not developed with regard to its durability, it becomes difficult for trust to thrive. Alternatively, forging long-term relationships provides opportunities for building employers' internal capacity to support and sustain workers with disabilities. It is only through developing these long-term relationships that true change in the job market will occur for persons with disabilities.

Service Competence

One of the clearest indicators regarding what employers look for in job placement agencies in terms of factors that ensure successful job placements is service competence. When a group of employers participating in the focus group described in the appendix was asked what it felt contributed most to successful employment outcomes for jobseekers with disabilities, "knowledgeable about business needs" was one of the most highly rated responses. Another prevalent response on the parts of employers in this group was "job placement personnel who understand job requirements." Out of over 100 responses, less than 10% of the employers surveyed mentioned jobseeker skills as a prerequisite for successful employment.

However, when asked what factors would help them achieve more successful job placements, job placement personnel tended to focus on increasing agency resources. For instance, the most frequently rated response in this regard was "more time," followed by "more money for job placement." Although scarcity of resources is a reality for many human services and job placement agencies, internal capacity is defined not only by the quantity of available resources, but also by the skill and competence levels of the personnel working within those agencies. Service competence—each partner perceiving the other as capable of making a worthwhile contribution—is critical in developing solid partnerships.

A Customer Service Orientation

Job placement agencies must remember that businesses are their customers. They are in the business of satisfying customers, just as are all service organizations. This realization was noticeably absent in early partnerships (described in Chapter 1). Yet, employers participating in the group study conducted by TransCen identified agency responsiveness as a key characteristic underlying successful job placements. A customer service orientation requires that agencies focus on satisfying the employers with whom they work rather than on the number of job placements made or the amount of funds received. Indeed, a customer service orientation highlights the reciprocal features and benefits to be gained by each party.

Table 2.1 lists the five key characteristics that are fundamental to the development of effective partnerships and an identifying element of each.

SATISFYING EACH OF YOUR CUSTOMERS

As is evident in Table 2.2, job placement agencies must simultaneously assess and respond to two sets of demands as they negotiate partnerships between employers and people with disabilities. For each set of demands, the intended outcome or benefit is reciprocal: the individual consumer receives a satisfactory job as the employer hires a satisfactory employee.

However, the process of satisfying these reciprocal demands requires a simultaneous internal/external balance that historically has been difficult for job placement agencies to achieve. This balance is frequently described as a successful job match—meeting the vocational goals of prospective employees by providing services that enable qualified workers to meet the requirements of prospective employers. As focus group research points out, employers want better access to qualified applicants with disabilities, whereas employees with disabilities generally demand access to employers who need their skills.

Satisfactorily achieving this internal/external balance necessitates a responsiveness to two sets of customer demands that ideally have matched sets of objectives.

The Employer as Customer

Employers are essentially customers of job placement agencies because they consume a service that job placement professionals offer. The ultimate service outcome is the successful employment of qualified individuals with disabilities in their businesses. To provide this benefit to businesses, job placement agencies must also meet other demands and needs of their customers regarding such things as workplace accommodation, job analysis, and environmental engineering. Indeed, job placement agencies mediate the relationship between employers and employees; they provide the bridge that results in meeting the employment needs of businesses.

Changes in the workforce can be seen as advantageous in this regard when job placement agencies help employers to see the benefits of investing in the human capi-

Table 2.1. The characteristics of successful partnerships

Partnership characteristics	Evidenced by
Trust	Understanding and respecting each other's needs
Goals and objectives that benefit everyone involved	Outcomes representing mutual risk and mutual gain
Long-term relationships	Ongoing contact and responsiveness
Service competence	Quality performance on each side
A customer service orientation	Customer satisfaction

Table 2.2. Service options and their benefits

Services needed by people with disabilities	Services needed by employers
Work adjustment training	Employees with good work skills
Career development	Employees who understand vocational interests
Jobsite training	Workplace skills
Job and task analysis	Job process mapping
Self-advocacy	Disability awareness; information regarding reasonable accommodation(s)
Vocational training	Skilled workforce

tal of the millions of individuals with disabilities who are not presently working. For instance, representatives of the Marriott Corporation approached TransCen seeking help in identifying new labor pools for their service-intensive industry. Recognizing that demographic trends indicated a shortage in one of their traditional labor pools—young people—they wanted a job placement professional to assist them in meeting their future business needs. However, they weren't interested in Marriott's traditional approach to hiring people with disabilities (i.e., relying on provider agencies to screen and train employees for jobs). Rather, they were interested in getting into the business of screening and training their own employees. After all, that's the way they built a very successful service industry over the past 65 years. Using existing human resource development and supervisory personnel, they set up an internal job training program that eventually succeeded in hiring many people with disabilities in selected areas throughout the United States.

Did the Marriott Corporation provide jobs for everyone who applied? Of course not; businesses always screen and hire according to labor needs and job requirements. Did they provide reasonable accommodations in the sense that they altered the work environment in order to hire a desirable employee or to retain and promote another? Yes, they did. However, these were business decisions, just as some businesses have begun to provide reasonable accommodations for single parents through on-site child-care programs. It's not a good deed; it's simply good business.

Marriott is disseminating these types of successful programs throughout the United States. How can these opportunities be exploited to develop partnerships? In answering this question, it is important to remember that successful workplace innovation exploits change as opportunity. Waiting for change to occur is what job placement professionals do when they expect companies simply to provide jobs for people with disabilities; it's all part of the so-called "beg, place, and pray" scenario. Exploiting change, by contrast, requires building partnerships in the workplace. In fact, this is what the most successful businesses do well.

The Client as Customer

People with disabilities are customers of job placement agencies because they, like employers, consume a service that these agencies offer. Again, the ultimate service outcome is successful employment for individuals with disabilities. In this case, job placement professionals must meet consumers' demands from an individual perspective, analyzing jobs based on employee preferences and available environmental resources. In this model of service delivery, the client is thus regarded as a consumer.

The first clear evidence of redefining or reframing the client in rehabilitation services in terms of his or her being the consumer came in the 1970s as part of a general paradigm shift in rehabilitation that focused attention on issues like choice and empowerment. Driving this process were the increasingly vocal demands of people with disabilities to control their own lives. The student uprising at Gallaudet University in 1988 (i.e., the students demanded the appointment of a new president who was deaf) provides a clear example of this political force. The passage of the Americans with Disabilities Act in 1990, after 5 years of effort on the parts of consumers and advocates alike, represents the culmination of a growing political force that emphasizes consumer empowerment.

Defining the service recipient as a consumer rather than as a client symbolizes a move away from the medical model of service delivery—based on explicit and implicit assumptions regarding functional deficits and professional expertise in assisting clients to adjust to their limitations—to one of empowerment that enables clients to gain or regain control over the external forces—service agencies, government regulations, and social attitudes—that affect their lives. Empowerment is a means of regaining control over life's events by placing choice, decision making, and responsibility in the hands of the consumer, in much the same way as they are integral to people's daily decisions to purchase goods or services in the private sector.

Accompanying these philosophical and social shifts embodied by the consumer movement were changes in federal legislation, service technologies, and service delivery. For instance, the Rehabilitation Act of 1973 mandated client participation in the development of individualized written rehabilitation plans (IWRPs), documents that specify services to be provided by state vocational rehabilitation agencies on behalf of consumers.

This legislative trend toward consumer involvement is even more evident in specific mandates incorporated into the Rehabilitation Act Amendments of 1992 (PL 102-569), particularly one that calls for each state to have an advisory council comprised of both citizens with disabilities and business representatives. Moreover, recent developments in service provision (e.g., supported employment) empower consumers by shifting the location of services from sheltered, segregated settings to competitive work environments where it is believed that people have greater latitude in determining and meeting their vocational goals.

One future trend that represents the capstone of consumerism is the demand for an individual "voucher system" to facilitate the purchase of job placement services. This voucher system would ideally enable consumers to shop for and buy those products and services that best meet their needs and promise the highest levels of quality and performance. Its philosophical bases are predicated on the ideas of choice and competition, thus forcing public agencies to be more accountable for quality by empowering service recipients to make choices.

Balancing the Needs of Employers and Consumers

For job placement agencies, satisfying both customers (i.e., employers and people with disabilities) is a complex balancing act. The agencies must continuously monitor external factors while refining and monitoring internal processes as new demands arise. For instance, regarding the consumer–customer relationship, as individual needs become increasingly demanding because of disability issues, additional service time may be required to meet these needs, thus resulting in a loss of available time to attend to employer's needs. Similarly, as job markets become more demanding or depressed, more time must be devoted to the employer–customer side of the balance, which also will cause uneven distribution of available resources.

All businesses are accustomed to a continuous monitoring process as they balance inputs against outcomes. Indeed, when a small business contemplates undertaking increased personnel costs in order to improve services, the decision must be based on an appropriate balance of inputs to outcomes. Quite simply, if the additional staff result in improved customer service, the decision to incur additional costs is beneficial. This principle, however simple, often is overlooked by job placement agencies.

Traditionally, decisions about increasing staff or incurring costs are based on internal factors. However, if a job placement agency is providing poor placements and is simultaneously working with a group of consumers with severe disabilities, more staff may be hired to manage disability issues. Nonetheless, more internal staff (viz., case managers or counselors) may not solve the problem, thus causing an improper balance between inputs and outcomes.

Similar problems may be created by the practice of hiring specialized personnel to conduct job placement activities. In some state job placement agencies, counselors attend to the consumer–customers, whereas specialized job development personnel deal with the employer–customers. This and other similar attempts to respond to the needs of both consumers and employers may prove effective so long as they are provided within a framework that incorporates a continuous monitoring process relevant to external as well as internal factors, circumstances, and demands. In other words, if counselors focus only on consumer issues, thereby ignoring the external environment in terms of local labor demands and/or specific employer needs for services, then specialized personnel represent an internally framed response to the external problem of providing jobs to people with disabilities. This issue requires attention not only to consumers' needs, but also to ensuring that consumers are assisted in making vocational choices that are feasible as well as relevant to real local labor market demands. This will in turn satisfy both customers, consumers as well as employers.

PRINCIPLES OF CUSTOMER SATISFACTION

What does customer satisfaction mean for service organizations? This section describes four critical components of customer satisfaction and reviews what each means to job placement personnel.

Principle #1: Customer satisfaction means providing quality services in order to ensure, as nearly as possible, that customers will have a positive reaction to a specific service encounter. How many times have you walked into a store and been met by a sullen salesperson who seems to feel that seeing you is the worst thing that has happened to him or her that day? How did that make you feel? Did you have a positive emotional reaction? Did you purchase anything despite the encounter? Chances are you didn't, unless the particular store was the only place that you could get what you needed, or unless other necessities such as time or energy invested influenced your decision. But, even if you did make a purchase, are you likely to return? Are you likely to tell your friends to shop at the same store?

Let's look at the same scenario in terms of employer relations and job development. Think of the last time you had contact with an employer for any reason. How quickly did you respond to the employer's concerns? How quickly did you return a phone call about a particular job problem or lead? Perhaps the employer had a question about the services your agency delivered. How did you respond? What if the employer said, "We don't usually hire people with disabilities"? What did you do? Did you deliver a lecture? Did you agree with the employer that some people with disabilities were not the best employees, but that, if given the chance, you could guarantee quality workers? What do you think the emotional reaction of the employer was to your interaction? What was your reaction?

Customer satisfaction is the result of performance. Basically, poor performance results in dissatisfaction, whereas good performance leads to heightened satisfaction.

Principle #2: The reactions that customers have to services influence their attitudes. For job placement agencies, customer reactions influence attitudes not only to particular agencies, but also to other job placement services, and even to people with disabilities in general. Negative reactions to service encounters elicit negative stereotypes regarding services, staff, and consumers. Unfortunately, negative encounters tend to be more often remembered and more frequently discussed by customers than do positive experiences. It is an old adage in marketing that a dissatisfied customer tells 20 people about his or her experience, but that a satisfied one tells only three.

Principle #3: Positive encounters over time determine perceptions of service quality. If employers perceive the benefits of services, they will likely return in the future. If you are satisfied with a particular contractor doing work on your house, you will both recommend that contractor to others and hire him or her again should the need arise. It should be obvious, however, that one successful job placement does not ensure positive encounters 100% of the time. It should be equally obvious that one unsuccessful job placement does not destroy a long-standing relationship. For example, a large grocery chain in the Washington, D.C., metropolitan area worked with TransCen for 3 years, employing over 50 students with disabilities making the transition from school to work. What sustained these relationships was certainly not the need for each of the students to be successful on the job, but rather the quality of services delivered by TransCen. Indeed, it is not individual employee failure that destroys a customer relationship; conversely, poor service performance over time is the factor that most damages employers' perceptions of service quality.

Principle #4: Service quality is a powerful determinant of customer satisfaction. This final principle reiterates the theme of this chapter—that partnerships depend on mutuality and trust, each of which is essential to fostering customer satisfaction. Here also the importance of monitoring service performance via customer outcomes rather than through internal standards is emphasized. Rewarding high performance based on outcomes is one of the essential conditions for shifting to a customer-driven model of service delivery.

CONCLUSION

It can no longer be business as usual. The chapters in this volume present practical strategies to facilitate dynamic partnerships between American businesses and job placement agencies. These partnerships call for relationships that are based on sound business practice as well as on the concept of job placement agencies being valuable technical advisors to employers as they respond to workforce challenges of the 21st century.

REFERENCES

Americans with Disabilities Act of 1990 (ADA), PL 101-336. (July 26, 1990). Title 42, U.S.C. 12101 et seq: *U.S. Statutes at Large, 104,* 327–378.

Rehabilitation Act of 1973, PL 93-112. (September 26, 1973). Title 29, U.S.C. 701 et seq: *U.S. Statutes at Large, 87,* 355–394.

Rehabilitation Act Amendments of 1992, PL 102-569. (October 29, 1992). Title 29, U.S.C. 701 et seq: *U.S. Statutes at Large, 106,* 4344–4488.

Chapter 3 _____

PREPARING FOR
EFFECTIVE PARTNERSHIPS

_____

Effective partnerships are built on reciprocity of power, decision making, and responsibility in achieving mutually beneficial outcomes. In order to achieve this fundamental exchange, any two partners, as customers to one another, must be able to determine what each: 1) has to offer to the other (features), and 2) needs and wants for itself (benefits). At the heart of this features-to-benefits approach is customer satisfaction, a concept discussed in Chapter 2 of this volume.

CONVERTING FEATURES INTO BENEFITS

After an entity's features are identified (i.e., what it has to offer), those features must be converted into benefits for a targeted partner. The importance of this features-to-benefits management orientation cannot be overemphasized, for it may determine the success of a given partnership; it can make or break strong ties between the business world and the human services profession.

According to Laura Davis, manager of community employment and training for Marriott Corporation:

> A relationship based on anything but that assumption of return on investment—be it based on "do it because it's right," "do it because it is charitable," "do it because we can get some decent PR"—is going to be a weak relationship. It's going to be weak because it will last as long as the business person continues to feel good about it, or charitable about it, or gets some decent PR. But as soon as times get tough it will fall apart. (L. Davis, personal communication, May, 1992)

Business partnerships are predicated on the idea that individual partners bring certain features to a partnership that are potentially beneficial to each of the other partners involved. It is likely that, as job placement professionals become increasingly adept at presenting their best features, and thus gain greater expertise in human resource management and accommodation, they will no longer be required to rely on weak partnership foundations such as those described above by Ms. Davis. In fact, both business and human services are gaining an increased appreciation of what each can bring to the other. "Business relationships, like others, are best when mutually beneficial. By providing employment opportunities for people with disabilities, we give people the opportunity to maximize their potential, while providing us the chance to build a well-qualified and committed workforce" (Marriott, 1992, p. 7). Indeed, this climate is conducive to developing the types of partnerships that will have enduring effect—partnerships that will elicit outcomes sought by both parties. There is tremendous potential: 1) for businesses to view job placement agencies as good sources of human capital, and 2) for job placement agencies to adopt sound business practices that lead to desired outcomes.

For these things to occur, job placement professionals must:

• Listen carefully to ascertain the needs and expectations of employers.
• Convey the features of their services.
• Present their features in terms of likely benefits to employers.

Traditionally, job placement agencies have presented to employers "work-ready, qualified applicants," and "access to various hiring incentives" (i.e., Targeted Jobs Tax Credit [TJTC]) as their primary features. However, focusing solely on these features relies on selling individual consumers rather than on selling services that are valuable and beneficial to employers as a whole. Included among the many features presently offered by job placement professionals are: expertise in occupational training, vocational evaluation, rehabilitation engineering, career counseling, job coaching, and monitoring, just to cite a few. The challenge for job placement professionals then becomes one of marketing the features of their services as benefits for employers, thereby shaping customer demand.

Lisa, an employment specialist at TransCen, is responsible for locating community jobs for students with significant disabilities who are making the transition from high school to work. Recently, she was able to schedule appointments with several large area companies both to discuss the types of services that she should provide and to inquire about the businesses' employment needs. During the course of her meetings with the human resource personnel at these companies, frequent reference was made to the Americans with Disabilities Act (ADA). Specifically, personnel officers indicated that they were confused and unsure regarding "reasonable accommodations." In a subsequent meeting with her supervisor, Lisa reported these visits, mentioning the confusion and concern that businesses had about the implementation of ADA regulations, especially with regard to reasonable accommodations. Lisa's supervisor wondered how she responded to these concerns. Lisa reported she had assured them that she would be there to make specific recommendations about reasonable accommodations should they work out any arrangements to hire students through TransCen. Her supervisor told her to immediately reschedule appointments with these organizations to offer them an introductory program regarding ADA and reasonable accommodations for people with disabilities. Although only one of these companies hired students, three purchased a training package comprising general disability awareness and ADA training from TransCen. Several consumers with disabilities have been hired by TransCen to assist in providing this training.

SHIFTING TO A MARKETING APPROACH TO SHAPE CUSTOMERS' DEMAND

As this discussion demonstrates, job placement agencies involved in the employment of people with disabilities have many beneficial features to offer employers. It is thus important that these agencies not only adopt a customer service orientation presenting features as benefits, but that they also shape customer demand for their services.

Shaping customer demand represents a fundamental step in marketing. As Peter Drucker (1985) suggests, marketing makes selling unnecessary because the end result is a willing customer. Retail stores regularly interact with their customers in this way.

Gibro Juarez was shopping for a compact disc (CD) player. In fact, he was buying one for the first time. Armed with a strong affinity for music but little knowledge about the various features of CD players, he walked into a large electronic appliance store. A sales associate quickly approached him and, learning of his desire to buy a CD player, began to recite the features of a top-of-the-line model on display. The sales associate recited information regarding such features as sound clarity, programming options, and remote control operation. It seemed to be what Gibro was looking for, but he declined to buy it after hearing the price. The sales associate simply shrugged and walked away.

About a week later, Gibro walked into another electronics store—a competitor of the first—and was again approached by a sales associate. Instead of reciting CD player features, this associate asked several questions: Do you listen to music for extended periods of time? Do you have a place for the CD player on a top shelf? In confined quarters? Do you like to listen to every song on an album or tape, or would you prefer to skip songs you don't like? The sales associate quickly ascertained that Gibro: 1) listened to music while reading or doing work and therefore did not want to keep changing discs, 2) had a place for the CD player on a spacious shelf and therefore could use a top loading model rather than one with a magazine loader, and 3) regularly fast forwarded tapes past songs that he didn't like.

The sales associate demonstrated a particular model having all the features that suited Gibro's needs and listening habits. It had a multi-disc, top loading carousel for hours of listening without changing CDs, and it was easy to program so unwanted songs could be easily eliminated. Even though it was relatively expensive like the one rejected at the first store, Gibro bought it.

Even the finest product will not be sold unless the buyer perceives some sort of benefit. Clearly, the first sales associate focused only on the CD player, never appealing to the customer's desires and expectations. The second sales associate was able to accomplish both and thus achieved a successful outcome.

As Mark McCormack (1984) so aptly suggests in his best-selling book on salesmanship, it's easier to get people to buy what they need than to get them to buy what you're selling. That is, correctly shaping and subsequently responding to your customers' needs is a key ingredient to developing mutually satisfying partnerships. Unfortunately, job placement professionals often discount the importance of responding to customers' needs in trying to ensure satisfaction.

Professionals must come to share a common vision regarding what defines quality performance and desired outcomes. Sharing an organizational vision necessitates that all personnel de-emphasize internal performance standards in lieu of measuring service outcomes via customer satisfaction. Customers base evaluations of services received on a variety of perceptions of both tangible and intangible indicators of performance. Returning a phone call to an employer is an example of a tangible performance indicator. However, it is also symbolic of customer responsiveness, which is perceived by the employer as being representative of service quality.

A review of business marketing literature coupled with the results of the focus group research outlined in the appendix indicate three necessary actions in order to shift to a marketing approach to shape customers' demand. These three key actions are:

1. Externalize agency services.
2. Deliver quality services.
3. Communicate effectively with consumers and employers.

Each is discussed in turn.

Externalize Agency Services

Throughout the 1980s, job placement agencies continued to provide clerical training for jobseekers using outdated electric equipment like typewriters. Not surprisingly, there was little demand for employees able to type 40 words per minute on an IBM Selectric. Futhermore, job placement staff often disdained or were intimidated by the business sector in their local communities when they attempted to identify local labor force needs. Similarly, they often were unaware of local economic forces and trends, and therefore developed services without paying attention to local labor market demands.

Services delivered to people with disabilities may be characterized as being highly individualized with a client-centered focus. The process of service delivery tends to focus on the internal system of service delivery rather than on environmental needs or labor market demands. As a result, local labor market demands typically do not shape the way in which services are delivered, and job placement personnel generally do not attempt to shape employers' demands for their services.

Focusing on internal service needs leads to avoidance; thus, every contact made with an area employer for the purpose of job development can be characterized as a "cold call." Consequently, job developers and employers still have little information about one another, and therefore have difficulty seeing how job placement services can be beneficial to businesses.

This type of internally driven organization is characteristic not only of job placement agencies, but of other human services agencies as well. The key driving these agencies is internal performance, not external forces such as local needs, customer satisfaction, or a changing economy. The relationship between process and outcome—between the delivery of services and the successful placement of people with disabilities in jobs—is often obscured. The benefits of services are realized in their actual delivery, not in outcomes subsequently achieved (i.e., jobs).

One of the frustrating aspects of an internally focused job placement agency is that failure to find sufficient or appropriate job placements for jobseekers frequently results in doubling job placement efforts rather than in refocusing attention on service outcomes. Although increased effort may be necessary, these heightened efforts are often oriented toward increasing internal resources, not toward improving external performance indicators. In other words, agencies search for solutions internally in order to explain and improve poor job placement performance. They look for more staff, money, time, and help. Although this is not inherently problematic, it makes no real effort to solve the overlying problem of poor employment outcomes. If employment outcomes are poor, how often do agencies ask their customers—jobseekers as well as employers—how they can improve services? How much time is spent examining the impressions that services and procedures create on the external environment? Conversely, how much time is spent trying to find ways to improve or increase internal resources as the sole response to poor outcomes?

This prevailing tendency to look internally is emphasized in the responses of job placement personnel who participated in the focus group outlined in the appendix. In response to the question, "How could you achieve greater success in job placement?", more than 50% of the responses began with the word "more"—more time for job development, more time to meet employers, more available entry-level jobs, more understanding on the parts of employers. Not one response regarded asking customers how services could be improved.

In contrast were employers' responses to the same question. As customers of job placement services, they responded by identifying standards of quality performance. They cited the need for agency personnel who: 1) were responsive to their needs, 2) were knowledgeable about their businesses, and 3) assisted with identifying reasonable accommodations. Although job placement professionals may want more internal resources, they will never achieve success without responding to customer demands. Indeed, customers are not interested in how many people it takes to run an agency; they care only about the quality of the results.

Why is this internal focus so characteristic of job placement agencies as compared to "for profit" businesses? Job placement agencies, which are similar to other public and nonprofit organizations, frequently experience a conflict in knowing whether to respond to internal needs (e.g., more services, increased allocations) or external demands (i.e., for qualified people and/or quality services). There are many reasons cited in literature to explain this conflict. As noted in Albin (1992) and Drucker (1985), there are many concerned parties involved in public service organizations. In job placement agencies, for instance, "concerned parties" may include clients, families, legislators, counselors, state agencies, and employers. Responding to individual demands can frequently lead to an overemphasis on internal approaches such as redesigning processes and operations rather than to external approaches that improve outcomes. Accreditation agencies, for example, tend to focus on internal criteria such as numbers of staff and types of services provided. Conversely, parents focus on the quality and caring of staff members. Agencies that become obsessed with these varied demands easily lose sight of external forces.

In many of these organizations, efficiency remains more highly valued than effectiveness. The ultimate goal of job placement agencies should be customer satisfaction —a qualitative outcome—rather than increasing quantities served—a quantitative outcome. Unfortunately, however, justification for additional budget allocations is based primarily on quantitative evidence (e.g., numbers served) rather than on qualitative evidence such as customer satisfaction. This fact is more apparent as resource cutbacks threaten service provision in dramatic ways. As a result, agency personnel tend to blame poor service performance on a lack of resources.

There is evidence, however, that suggests that these attitudes are changing. As resources become more scarce, public agencies are becoming aware of that which successful private sector businesses have long known—that the marketplace will not enlist their services unless they provide a high-quality product. Therefore, public agencies are starting to promote their services in efforts to increase utilization. The use of marketing tools like brochures that advertise services, public service advertisements regarding how agencies can address employer needs, and employer sensitivity training seminars are all examples of externally focused efforts.

However, it is important to note that promotional techniques or marketing tools do not sell services. Rather, customer satisfaction ultimately sells services. Similarly, promotional techniques do not create a demand for services; quality performance does. Indeed, refocusing programs toward the external environment requires a commitment to continuous quality improvement to shape customer demands to fit organizational goals. Essentially, this means adopting what may be described as a marketing rather than a selling orientation to the delivery of goods and services.

Various influences and trends existing today lend emphasis to the need for job placement agencies to embrace an external orientation. These influences include the Americans with Disabilities Act, the changing demography of the United States, and the new flexibility of employers in meeting employee needs in the workplace. The following sections outline the basic principles at work in externally focused agencies.

Focus on Quality Outcomes, Not Quantitative Inputs   Quality outcomes concern customer satisfaction—both with regard to the employer–customer and the consumer–customer. Each must derive satisfaction from service encounters. The issue is not the quantity of persons placed, nor is it the vast array of new service delivery technologies that will ostensibly result in placement. Rather, the issue is how well services satisfy customers. Indeed, the evaluation of services should be measured by quality not quantity.

Shape Public Awareness of Products and Services   So-called "spin doctors" often shape the public's perceptions of political candidates. In a similar fashion, shaping customers' expectations of an agency's services is directly related to their perceptions of that agency. As Table 3.1 indicates, customers' reactions are the result of varying expectations of the services being received.

Indeed, the social climate of the 1990s creates opportunities to shape awareness of and demand for job placement services. Job placement agencies are taking advantage of businesses' heightened awareness of workers with disabilities by: 1) offering ADA and disability awareness training, 2) increasing the visibility of services and their benefits, and 3) taking advantage of the benefits of hiring people with disabilities as a means of building an enriched and inclusive corporate culture. For example, TransCen has established a partnership with a large human resource development training firm in which TransCen will assist in delivering diversity training seminars for employers. Recognizing the need to include persons with disabilities in the workforce, TransCen subsequently developed a workshop designed to: 1) improve awareness of disability issues, and 2) devise strategies for improving organizational commitment and responsiveness to employees with disabilities.

In this way, TransCen was able to shape public awareness regarding its services. Similarly, it pays for job placement agencies to actively participate in community activities that may seem to have no direct relationship to their missions. Indeed:

Table 3.1.   Expectations shape reactions

	Deliver low	Deliver high
Low expectations	So who cares?	I can't believe this!
High expectations	This is a nightmare.	Keep it up (and you better).

- A healthy community means a healthy business climate.
- A healthy business climate creates more jobs.
- Community activities provide opportunities to network with people and expand contact among members of various disciplines.
- Interacting with the larger community keeps job placement agencies from becoming too insular.
- Businesses—job placement agencies should, after all, consider themselves businesses—and the community ultimately have a shared future.

Table 3.2 provides several examples of activities that agencies can use to externalize their services.

Monitor the Quality of Services Monitoring the quality of services is critical to an external orientation. This monitoring can be accomplished in a variety of ways, for example, through focus groups or employer surveys.

Essentially, two questions must be answered in monitoring job placement services: 1) How aware are people of service delivery? 2) How do customers evaluate those services? These two questions form the basis for the matrix shown in Figure 3.1.

The horizontal axis refers to visibility of services. This awareness can fall anywhere along the indicated continuum. The representative points depend on individual definitions of service saturation. That is, if the goal is to make all employers in the local labor market aware of employment-based services, and only 30% of them have heard of a specific job placement agency, the awareness factor is low for that agency. However, if the goal is to limit public awareness (during a period of reorganization, for instance), and a sample of potential consumers reveals that 50% of them are aware of that agency, this percentage is relatively high.

Attitudes toward services are less likely to have variable endpoints because it is desirable for people to have positive attitudes toward job placement agencies and their services. However, strategies designed to promote increased awareness and/or positive changes in attitude may be required. If visibility is low but attitudes are high regarding a specific agency (quadrant 2), then that agency should direct its efforts toward increasing visibility through mass marketing and promotional strategies. However, if visibility is high with poor attitudes, then strategies should be directed toward quality enhancement or service improvement, not toward extensive public relations campaigns.

Quadrant #1: High Visibility/Positive Attitudes This is of course the ideal quadrant, but it doesn't allow agencies to rest on past achievements. Leverage your success by initiating new business ventures (e.g., employer training regarding disability issues in the workplace), by redesigning services to respond to changing environmental demands, or by investing in new partnerships.

Quadrant #2: Low Visibility/Positive Attitudes Like quadrant #1, this is a promising quadrant in which to be. It indicates the delivery of quality services, but with less

Table 3.2. Externalizing services: Examples of activities

- Solicit input from area employers.
- Ask businesses about their needs; develop services that are responsive to those needs.
- Provide communication skills training to staff.
- Read business pages in local papers to find out what regional and local employers are saying and doing.
- Become visible in the local labor and business communities.
- Sponsor and take part in various charitable events; being a nonprofit agency does not preclude making social contributions to the community.

Positive attitudes

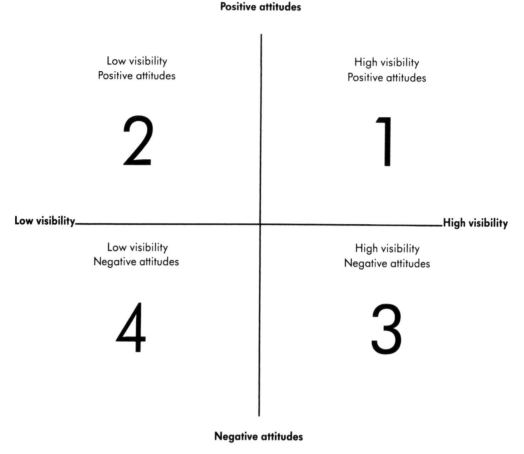

Figure 3.1. Agency visibility and public awareness.

promising public awareness. Heightening awareness involves increasing public information through public service messages, newsletters to area employers, testimonials from satisfied employers, and greater saturation in the marketplace. Distributing such information may be facilitated by: attending community business meetings, belonging to local chambers of commerce, sponsoring various charitable events in the community, and ensuring that staff members have business cards to distribute at every public event.

Quadrant #3: High Visibility/Negative Attitudes   Quadrant #3 is probably the most difficult quadrant in which to be, and the one that requires the most intensive remedial activity. Focus groups may help here—enlisting the help of business leaders, families, and consumers to brainstorm about how to best improve services. The investment of time in assessing the quality of services offered is critical. How well trained are staff? How knowledgeable are they about job placement practices? Use resources related to continuous quality improvement such as Albin (1992) both to assess services and to problem solve for change.

Quadrant #4: Low Visibility/Negative Attitudes   This quadrant represents a position similar to that of Quadrant #3, but the agency is not dealing with pervasive public awareness. In other words, few people are aware of the poor services being provided. Focus groups that address specific problems may be helpful in initiating program overhaul, both internally and externally. It may be useful to identify and review the agency's performance indicators while maintaining this low profile. Then, invest in a program of continuous quality improvement in order to solve the problems plaguing the agency.

Deliver Quality Services

Employers do not purchase programs; they purchase benefits (i.e., an employee who can perform a job or service that responds to identified employer needs). When employers purchase services from a job placement agency—hiring a consumer of the agency's employment service or having the agency assist in identifying reasonable accommodations—they infer critical factors about that agency based on perceptions of the quality of the benefits. College students evaluate professors based not on the number of degrees or credentials they have, but on how well they convey course material. Similarly, employers evaluate services offered by job placement agencies based not on the individual qualifications of staff who administer those services, but on how satisfactorily the services correspond to their needs.

This evaluative mechanism, and the criteria used to assess quality, was made clear by the employers who participated in the focus group research outlined in the appendix. They suggested that successful job placements occur when job placement staff: follow up on job performance, have positive attitudes even when problems are evident, and return phone calls.

Ensuring that employers perceive the quality and value of an intangible service necessitates that these services appear tangible to those employers. Because inferences regarding service quality are based on the visible, measurable components of agencies, steps to ensure that these components reflect quality are critical to shaping perceptions. In marketing management research, the process of managing customers' perceptions of service quality is referred to as "impression management" (Crane, 1991).

Impression management shapes the way that customers infer information about service quality, and is based on four key organizational elements: physical environment, people, procedures, and organizational capabilities. Each is discussed in turn.

Physical Environment—Creating an Environment that Elicits Desired Impressions Job placement agencies differ with regard to physical environment. For example, in many agencies, consumers participate in a variety of on-site activities such as vocational evaluation or work adjustment training. Other agencies may not sponsor on-site programs; instead, services are delivered where they are needed. Examples of this include supported employment programs in which job coaches are stationed at work-sites and residential programs in which staff only work in homes. Nonetheless, service users and potential users frequently have an opportunity to visit agencies, and their impressions of the physical environment are critical to attitudes about agency services.

People—Internal Marketing It is a trite slogan in the field of job placement that the people who work best with consumers are not necessarily those who work best with employers. This concept reflects a common misperception of agencies and staff regarding the importance of internal marketing. Indeed, in order to effectively market services externally, services must be effectively marketed internally.

Employees who are confused about organizational objectives—those who regard results as secondary to service delivery—will fail to meet the external expectations of employers, and will thus fail in meeting the internal expectations of agency management and staff. Agencies need to present their expectations internally as aggressively as they market them externally. As one marketing researcher puts it, "Internal marketing involves creating an organizational climate that leads to the right service personnel performing the right service in the right way" (Crane, 1991, p. 11).

A staff's dress and demeanor have a lot to do with this concept of internal marketing. If an agency is truly interested in developing partnerships, then staff members who dress informally or an internal environment characterized by chaos and sloppiness implicitly forces an agency to be devoted more to internal standards than external performance. Remember, it is difficult for job placement professionals to market an agency's services based on quality and mutual benefit when its program and staff do not subscribe to the same mission.

Procedures   Neither would-be employees nor potential employers will have patience for lengthy service delays, extended procedures, or excessive red tape. Unfortunately, one of the realities of public and nonprofit service delivery is the existence of regulatory conditions that often result in excessive procedural delays. However, an effective manager can mitigate harsh perceptions of these procedures by ensuring that customers are kept informed regarding anticipated delays, by being responsive to customers' frustrations during periods of delay, and by doing everything possible to guarantee that delays do not result from excessively convoluted bureaucratic inefficiency. Promptly returning phone calls as well as responding positively to, and demonstrating respect for, employers as well as jobseekers are all methods of ensuring that agency procedures do not have a negative impact on perceptions of service quality.

Organizational Capabilities   An organization with an established, tangible track record of quality performance is likely to be successful in the future. Tangible evidence of quality performance includes such things as testimonials, having employers confirm claims regarding quality service, an organizational resumé listing specific agency accomplishments that are suited to particular customer demands, and agency newsletters.

Have you ever hired a contractor to work on your house? Several may bid on the job, but most people are likely to hire the one who provides the best visible demonstration of his or her organizational capability. For contractors, a list of satisfied customers provides this type of visual evidence of service performance.

Managing consumers' impressions of job placement agencies may seem to suggest that indicators of organizational performance are superficial. That is, as long as services and benefits are perceived as being of high quality, their actual effectiveness is irrelevant. Test this faulty supposition by asking yourself what happened the last time you bought something that looked great, but fell apart after being used. Satisfaction with the product's superficial quality subsequently waned, and your feelings toward the manufacturer and the store that sold it to you probably did not remain very positive.

The point here is that superficiality will not fool anyone. Indeed, tangible evidence of service quality is one of the quality performance indicators on which customers judge job placement agencies, and they will not be easily fooled.

Communicate Effectively with Consumers and Employers

Effective communication is also essential if an agency is to develop an efficient marketing approach to service provision. Indeed, effective communication is the basis for all relationships, and partnerships are necessarily relationships.

Effective communication involves responsive listening—the ability to solve problems in responding to the demands or complaints of individual customers. The

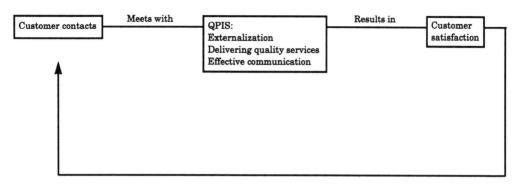

Figure 3.2. Job placement agencies and their customers.

focus group research in the appendix demonstrates the importance of responsive listening to both jobseekers and employers. Both groups emphasize such basic skills as returning phone calls, responding quickly to requests, and avoiding social service jargon. If a service is poor, a placement doesn't work out, or a customer is dissatisfied, active and responsive listening may be the key to re-establishing felicitous relations.

CONCLUSION

Figure 3.2 illustrates the circular relationship existent between customers and job placement agencies. The quality performance indicators (QPIs)—externalization, delivering quality services, and effective communication—facilitate customer satisfaction. It should be noted that providing customer satisfaction requires a shift in the direction of agency functions from inputs and internal processes to external conditions and qualitative outcomes. In other words, QPIs ensure that partnerships are based on mutual investment and therefore result in mutually beneficial outcomes— the goal of successful partnerships.

REFERENCES

Albin, J. (1992). *Quality improvement in employment and other human services*. Baltimore: Paul H. Brookes Publishing Co.

Crane, F.G. (1991). A practical guide to professional services marketing. *Journal of Professional Services Marketing, 5*(1), 3–16.

Drucker, P. (1985). *Innovation and entrepreneurship*. New York: Harper & Row.

Marriott, J. W. (1992). *Bridges from school to work: A project of the Marriott Foundation for people with disabilities*. (Available from TransCen, Inc., 451 Hungerford Drive, Suite 700, Rockville, MD 20850.)

McCormack, M.H. (1984). *What they don't teach you at Harvard Business School*. New York: Bantam Books.

Chapter 4 _____

PARTNERSHIPS AT WORK

TransCen was established in 1986 in order to research, design, and implement innovations that would specifically ensure better school-to-work transitions for young people with disabilities as well as to promote the employment of people with disabilities in general. In pursuing this mission, TransCen discovered that aggressive action was required if dismal unemployment rates for people with disabilities were to be improved. What follows are three case studies describing partnerships between Trans-Cen and various employers. Each reflects the features-to-benefits concept and demonstrates collaboration predicated upon mutual return on investment.

CASE STUDY #1: THE SOUTHLAND EXPERIENCE

In 1988, the Southland Corporation was experiencing a severe labor shortage in its Washington, D.C., market area. With an area-wide unemployment rate of just over 2%, virtually everyone without significant barriers to employment had jobs. Southland's efforts to recruit employees for the 7–11 convenience store chain through traditional means—newspaper ads, career fairs, even "help wanted" signs—were failing miserably. Vacancies went months without being filled. A great deal of money, staff time, and company resources were being spent on a seemingly unsolvable problem. One Southland manager put it this way: "We just couldn't keep up; some employees were working double and even triple shifts" (S. Bartley, personal communication, June, 1989).

Early Recruitment Attempts: Where Were the Workers?

Southland's situation became so tenuous that a position was created within its personnel department devoted solely to recruiting so-called "nontraditional jobseekers." This person was effectively given the responsibility of engaging the local employment and training system (i.e., Job Training Partnership Act, vocational rehabilitation, job services, and programs with similar purposes) to stimulate Southland's recruitment and hiring process. An aggressive outreach effort was subsequently launched, and the division recruiter (as this person was called) contacted and developed relationships with numerous employment and training programs in the Washington, D.C., metropolitan area.

These relationships resulted in successful placements for those few individuals who were assisted in their job preparation and search by involved employment and training professionals. However, these situations were often characterized by relatively short job tenures for those hired.

"We were able to get people with disabilities into some stores using agency job coaches in some cases, but until later we could not keep them for very long and we still had a lot of jobs to fill," said Spencer Bartley, Southland's division recruiter (personal communication, June, 1989). Essentially, the few placements in relation to the hundreds of vacancies had virtually no effect on the continuing labor shortage that Southland was experiencing.

In effect, job placement agencies were given the opportunity to scour their lists of clients in finding candidates to fill vacancies presented by a receptive job market. This was a potentially productive situation for job placement personnel to provide placements for qualified candidates. Southland found, however, that qualified, job-ready applicants were just not easy to find, despite its aggressive recruitment outreach.

Jobseekers with Disabilities: Where Were the Jobs?

At about the same time that the Southland Corporation launched its intensive recruitment efforts, the Montgomery County, Maryland, public school system was taking a serious look at postsecondary employment outcomes for young people with disabilities who had completed school. Their conclusions were bleak at best. At a time when the area was experiencing a severe labor shortage, less than 50% of the area's special education graduates were employed in any capacity 2 years after leaving school (Hawkins, 1987).

What factors contributed to this dilemma? First, despite both a comprehensive curricular emphasis on workplace preparation and an agreement between the local school and vocational rehabilitation systems, not all students were willing to continue in a system for which eligibility was contingent on identification as a person with a disability. For instance, in order to maintain services upon leaving school, students with learning disabilities were required to apply for and subsequently be determined to be eligible to receive services through the state vocational rehabilitation agency. Thus, referral to vocational rehabilitation to be further assessed, categorized, and labelled as having a learning disability was not considered an attractive alternative by many young people (Tilson, Taymans, & Germino-Hausken, 1991).

Second, students whose disabilities were not apparent often found it relatively easy to obtain an entry level job. However, they faced a high probability of failure on the job unless specific and individualized accommodations were provided (Neubert, Tilson, & Ianacone, 1989). In fact, some studies of postsecondary outcomes for individuals with learning disabilities who received special education services have shown that, in addition to job failure, the possibilities of poverty and in some cases contact with the criminal justice system are also notably heightened (Wagner, 1991).

An Emerging Partnership

Southland sought help from TransCen because of its inability to locate a suitable labor pool. School system personnel also contacted TransCen concerning the continuing dismal employment outcomes of students with learning disabilities.

TransCen considered the frustrations of both employers who had difficulty locating workers through existing job placement programs and young people with learning disabilities who encountered continuing difficulty maintaining employment. As a result, TransCen and Southland formed a partnership to develop a prototype employee assistance program for workers with learning disabilities.

With a seed grant from the National Center on Learning Disabilities, TransCen assisted Southland in creating a position within its personnel department. This employee assistance specialist (EAS) was charged with these basic responsibilities:

- Screen applicants referred by high school special education teachers and job placement agencies.
- Identify job openings for these young people in local 7–11 stores.
- Match applicants to job openings.
- Train new hires in their jobs.
- Identify and incorporate accommodations for these new hires.
- Provide follow up as necessary.

Critical Departure from Traditional Job Placement Roles

The employee assistance specialist was employed by Southland and reported to the director of personnel. Her first loyalty, therefore, was to the company. She was thoroughly trained and acquainted with the company's training procedures, and was familiar with its needs and expectations.

A major responsibility was identified at the outset: providing ongoing training to all managers and supervisors involved or potentially involved with new hires. Thus, expertise in hiring, training, managing, and accommodating workers would be internalized in the company; continued reliance on outside job placement services would thus be minimized.

During the first 2 years of the project, two critical roles of the EAS were: 1) to provide awareness training to management personnel concerning the nature of learning disabilities, and 2) to provide on-site instruction to supervisors and store managers about specific accommodations for employees with learning disabilities. Concomitantly, it was TransCen's responsibility to provide training and consultation services to the EAS regarding disability awareness and reasonable accommodations.

Her role as the company's designated "disability trainer and expert" has continued. In fact, she has extended her responsibilities within the company far beyond the originally conceived parameters of the project. It is clear that expertise in the fields of rehabilitation and disability awareness no longer rests exclusively with outside job placement professionals. As a human resource development specialist at Southland puts it, "Equipping our company to adequately manage the diversity that exists in our present and future workforce is a major priority. Understanding disability and developing confidence and competence in supervising employees with disabilities are important tools of human resource management" (M. Wilner, personal communication, August, 1989).

Outcomes

This 2-year pilot was extremely successful for both TransCen and Southland. Forty-four persons with learning disabilities were hired by Southland; their average tenure was three times that of typical Southland employees holding similar positions. In fact, several were promoted to management positions. In addition, the EAS continued to be employed by Southland, and people with learning disabilities continued to be hired and accommodated (Luecking, Tilson, & Wilner, 1991).

Not only were benefits measurable in terms of numbers of people placed, but other more enduring benefits resulted from this project as well. First, a considerable amount of knowledge about the internal workings of Southland's corporate structure and personnel processes was gained. The value of having intimate knowledge of corporate operations has been critical in the potential development of new partnerships with other companies. Second, while filling a human resource need, Southland gained a great deal of expertise and knowledge regarding the accommodation of employees with learning and other disabilities. This in turn represented a benefit to all employees with disabilities subsequently hired by Southland.

Early in Southland's pilot project, a store manager attended a training presentation on learning disabilities given by the employee assistance specialist (EAS). After learning that some people with learning disabilities have trouble reading, he approached the EAS about a particular problem he was having with one of his employees. A young man who worked as a store clerk in his store was doing an excellent job and he wanted to promote him to assistant store manager. However, he failed the required written test for the promotion four times. The manager wondered if there was a school to which the clerk could go to learn to read better.

After meeting the clerk, the EAS discovered that he read with difficulty because of an identified learning disability, but that he knew well the information necessary to be considered for the promotion. The EAS arranged to have the test administered orally. The clerk thereafter passed with one of the highest scores and was immediately promoted. Making this relatively simple accommodation thus added to Southland's growing expertise in disability management in the workplace.

As in any business partnership, you must be able to convert each party's features into tangible benefits. In the partnership between Southland and TransCen, features and benefits were clearly identified, and this led to a mutual return on investment, as illustrated in Tables 4.1 and 4.2.

CASE STUDY #2: THE MARRIOTT EXPERIENCE

In 1988, the predictions of the Hudson Institute's *Workforce 2000* study were already evident for the Marriott Corporation. A labor-short economy was making it increasingly difficult to attract and retain entry-level workers. The local government even mobilized the Montgomery County Entry/Re-entry Employment Task Force to recommend strategies to assist businesses with this problem. One recommended strategy of this task force was the expanded use of the local employment and training system. The programs therein comprised are offered to private industries by state and federal mandates and are designed to improve employment opportunities for workers with

Table 4.1. TransCen's features as benefits for Southland

Features of TransCen	Converted to	Benefits for Southland
• Access to applicants with learning disabilities		• Increased applicant pool
• Knowledge of accommodations for people with learning disabilities		• Increased supervisory expertise/ increased employee retention
• Access to funding sources		• Money
• Knowledge of financial incentives for hiring people with disabilities		• Money
• Consultation		• Reduced training costs

Table 4.2. Southland's features as benefits for TransCen

Features of Southland	Converted to	Benefits for TransCen
• Available jobs		• Employment of people with learning disabilities
• Employee assistance program		• Accommodations for applicants
• Personnel training system		• Supervisors who were sensitive to disability issues
• Well-delineated personnel structure		• Increased insight into corporate mode of operation

disabilities by increasing incentives to businesses to hire and train them. However, making use of these various programs is frequently complicated, which in turn discourages all but the largest and/or most persistent employers. Therefore, the challenge to Marriott and other employers was to make sense of the vast and complicated network of available programs and incentives.

Human Resource Problems Mount

Marriott reported having some success in working with this complicated network of vocational service programs. "The corporation had been looking at alternative applicant sources for some time . . . in a fairly unfocused way. There appeared to be some real opportunity in the area of people with disabilities," according to Mark Donovan, the manager of community employment and training for Marriott Corporation at that time (personal communication, December, 1992). However, as with most other employers, Marriott was largely unable to manage and accommodate applicants with disabilities without considerable assistance from external agencies.

One of the newer job placement services that promised an avenue for ongoing employment assistance for workers with disabilities was supported employment. This service was beginning to receive considerable attention, especially in the service industry (Lieberman, 1989).

Supported employment, which emphasizes continuous on-the-job support provided through a job coach employed by a job placement agency or vocational service program, was potentially beneficial to employers like Marriott because it opened a whole new applicant pool by providing workers with disabilities with on-the-job training and support. Regardless, according to Luecking (1990), when asked about supported employment, Marriott and other employers cited several concerns:

• External agencies were often unfamiliar with company needs.
• Job coach quality was often low.
• Job coach turnover was too frequent.
• Job coaches were often intrusive to the work environment.
• External administrative/bureaucratic requirements were often perplexing.
• When job coaches were absent, supervisors and co-workers were not properly prepared to manage and supervise supported employees.

Interestingly, these same concerns often have been cited in professional literature as concerns of job placement services in general (Mank, Buckley, & Rhodes, 1990; Nisbet & Hagner, 1988; Trach & Rusch, 1989).

Out of necessity, Marriott was willing to consider hiring people with disabilities who required considerable on-the-job support. However, they recognized the need to develop their internal capacity to provide the necessary support to these workers. What was needed, according to Mark Donovan, was "a project that really gave us an opportunity to develop that expertise internally and to get a stronger buy-in" (M. Donovan, personal communication, December, 1992).

A Partnership Emerges

One strategy that addressed the problems involved with traditional supported employment enlisted the features-to-benefits model—taking the best features of supported employment and translating them into benefits for employers. Conversely, the best features of company training and management were translated into benefits for jobseekers with disabilities. In effect, the challenge was to demonstrate ways that employers could assume greater responsibility for, and become more expert at, managing and accommodating workers with disabilities who required more than typical amounts of on-the-job support.

The stage was set for the development of a new kind of partnership. Several questions were asked regarding the funding situation and the needs of employers. Why not, as was done in the Southland example, teach employers how to recruit, select, train, and manage workers with significant disabilities? This certainly seemed appropriate given the increasing pressure to better use a shrinking labor pool that included a growing diversity of applicants. Alternatively, why not expand employment opportunities for people with disabilities using present funding in new and creative ways?

With these questions in mind, TransCen approached Marriott with the following proposal: "We will pay you to try a new approach in hiring and accommodating people with disabilities."

The Partnership's Parameters

After considerable negotiation, an agreement was reached that set the parameters for a 2-year demonstration project to be funded by the Maryland State Planning Council on Developmental Disabilities. This funding was secured in large part because the proposed partnership had tremendous potential to effect system-wide change. Essentially, Marriott agreed to:

- Hire 16 people with developmental disabilities.
- Pay them at least minimum wage and provide benefits congruous to those of other company employees.
- Enlist a Marriott employee as a full-time job trainer.
- Continue the program if it proved to be beneficial to company operations.
- Help disseminate the results of the project.

TransCen agreed to:

- Pay Marriott sufficient money (from the Council's funding) to cover the costs of the job trainer's salary and his or her fringe benefits for 2 years.
- Help recruit applicants with developmental disabilities.
- Assist in the selection and subsequent matching of workers based on individual characteristics and specific job requirements.
- Provide technical assistance to the job trainer and other corporate personnel, especially managers and supervisors, in how to support (i.e., accommodate and manage) people with disabilities.
- Assist in evaluating the project at its conclusion.

TransCen helped Marriott to identify an individual (then employed as a personnel recruiter at a local Marriott Hotel) to be the job trainer. Although she had no previous experience in working with people with disabilities, she had worked for the corporation for several years in various capacities. Therefore, she was well acquainted with Marriott's corporate structure. With the assistance of TransCen she eventually learned about recruiting, selecting, training, and supporting workers with disabilities.

The first job trainer employed by the Marriott Corporation for the 2-year demonstration project was promoted to human resource manager at a Marriott Hotel after only 9 months. She has now become the regional director of human resources for Marriott's Residence Inn, which serves the entire western United States. This is a career path available to few employment program or job placement specialists. It is, however, quite advantageous for job applicants with disabilities to have a knowledgeable, experienced person providing direction within a whole network of hotel properties. She herself recently confirmed this when she stated at a National Symposium for Supported Employment Professionals: "Now that I've done it, I can share with Marriott managers how relatively uncomplicated it can be to hire, train, and accommodate employees with disabilities" (Myers, 1992).

Outcomes

As planned, 16 people were hired and supported during the designated 2-year period. All were paid at least minimum wage, although most were paid the prevailing wages for the positions for which they were hired. Twelve remained employed upon the conclusion of the project. These individuals averaged in excess of 34 hours per week; their average wage was $4.19 per hour (the minimum wage at that time was $3.75 per hour).

As a result of this project, Marriott received tax credits and on-the-job training subsidies. In addition, the project elicited considerable positive publicity, including a front page feature in the *New York Times*. Marriott also gained considerable expertise in managing workers with disabilities. This is evidenced not only by continuation of the project, but also by its subsequent replication in other regions.

According to Kathleen Alexander, vice president of personnel services for Marriott:

> The cornerstone of the Marriott/TransCen Project was the utilization of an internal Marriott job trainer. In past projects, we had often worked with job trainers provided by the rehabilitation agencies, with varying degrees of success. The Marriott internal trainer was able to bring to the project a strong knowledge of our company policies and procedures and the ability to interact with management, which increased the new employee's chances for success.

Laurie Patterson Axtell, a job trainer with Marriott, echoes this perspective: "I was already employed by Marriott, so I knew the company's goals" (TransCen, Inc., 1989).

Not to be underestimated is the benefit that TransCen gained through its close association with a respected corporate entity. TransCen's personnel learned the values associated with the "corporate culture," developed an appreciation for the best features of corporate human resources management, and translated theory into bottom-line action. Tables 4.3 and 4.4 illustrate the features-to-benefits model for TransCen and Marriott.

Table 4.3. TransCen's features as benefits for Marriott

Features of TransCen	Converted to	Benefits for Marriott
• Knowledge of developmental disabilities		• Technical assistance in accommodation
• Access to jobseekers with developmental disabilities		• Employees
• Grantwriting expertise/ access to funding sources		• Money
• Training expertise		• Increased training skills
• Consultation		• Increased confidence in employing people with disabilities

This initiative continues in its original location in Maryland, and is funded through a combination of Targeted Jobs Tax Credits (TJTCs), On-the-Job Training (OJT) subsidies, and Job Training Partnership Act (JTPA) training dollars. More than 50 individuals have been employed since the initiation of the project in 1989. They are truly the beneficiaries of this partnership.

Critical Questions

Two critical and recurring questions were asked both before and since this collaboration was initiated:

1. How could it be ensured that Marriott or any large corporation would follow through on such a project once the start-up money from the Maryland Planning Council on Developmental Disabilities ran out?
2. Why couldn't a large corporate entity such as Marriott pay for such a project themselves if they really believed in it?

Each is discussed in turn.

The Value of Employees with Disabilities   The first question is really grounded in skepticism: would any large corporate employer have a continuing interest in hiring and retaining people with disabilities after support and financial incentives were gone? Implicit in this question is the underlying attitude that these employees are unlikely to be valued by the business community. However, quite the opposite occurred in this partnership, as evidenced by expansion of the original project and high employee retention rates.

Table 4.4. Marriott's features as benefits for TransCen

Features of Marriott	Converted to	Benefits for TransCen
• Jobs		• Employment for people with developmental disabilities
• Knowledge of how jobs are performed		• Refinement of precision training and job analysis procedures
• Knowledge of the company's culture		• Ability to match aspects of company culture to jobseekers' preferences and temperaments
• Attention to bottom line		• Long-term return on initial investment
• Profit motive		• Modeling effective business practices
• Customer service orientation		• Outcome orientation
• History of business success		• Association with a winner

Mutual Return on Investment The second question demonstrates a basic misunderstanding of the nature of business and the concept of mutual return on investment. Logic dictates that, unless there is a way of gaining the revenues necessary to cover the costs of hiring a job coach or trainer, there is no way that such a person could be retained. Therefore, companies must consider the revenue-producing potential of new employees. Businesses have always spent money purposefully. Even the philanthropic efforts of corporations often reflect their interest in gaining a business advantage over competitors. However, this question reflects the viewpoint that job placement agencies and the people thereby served should be *beneficiaries* of corporate America; this is not mutual return on investment.

> Job placement services more often characterize themselves as human service agencies than as potential business partners. Unconsciously, by focusing on disability issues, the impression is often given that what is expected of employers is a gesture of good will and that employment programs need businesses more than businesses need employment programs. As a result, job placement programs are most often relegated to a subordinate role in relationships with businesses and employers. Not only is this a distinct disadvantage to developing jobs, but it is an inadvertent devaluation of job-seekers with disabilities as well. Indeed, a good cause does not necessarily make one a good partner.

With the help of the grant from the Council on Developmental Disabilities, TransCen invested over $50,000 in Marriott (which covered the job trainer's salary and fringe benefits) during the 2-year demonstration project. Many people would be appalled at the thought of a nonprofit organization giving this much money to a corporate giant. However, the most successful partnerships are predicated on mutual return on investment.

Not only is this project continuing to provide Marriott with qualified workers, but it has also become the building block for a broader-based partnership. It is because of this project that several Marriott executives later invited TransCen to assist in the development of the *Bridges . . . from school to work* program. Therefore, the initial $50,000 investment led to the development of a program that enables TransCen to help over 200 people a year become employed in over 120 different companies in the greater Washington, D.C., area. This is obviously quite a substantial return on investment for both Marriott and TransCen.

CASE STUDY #3: *BRIDGES . . . FROM SCHOOL TO WORK*

The previous case studies illustrate the point that innovative approaches can be implemented successfully with large corporate employers. However, because the majority of employers in the United States are small businesses, one might wonder how job placement professionals and businesspeople apply these same concepts with small and mid-sized employers. This case study provides an example in this regard. As will be seen, employers of all sizes and descriptions are presently collaborating to build upon the features-to-benefits concept in looking to ensure mutual return on investment for all parties.

In 1989, the Marriott family—the founders and directors of Marriott Corporation—sought to develop a new focus regarding one aspect of their philanthropic pursuits. Their goal was to develop a dynamic business–community partnership that would capitalize on both the Corporation's experience employing people with disabilities and the family's commitment to community philanthropy. The dual thrust of this venture was to: 1) educate businesses in creatively and successfully utilizing the human resources of people with disabilities, and 2) benefit young people with disabilities exiting secondary school programs. The Marriott Foundation for People with Disabilities was formed to oversee this venture.

A Partnership Formed to Implement the *Bridges* Program

To further refine initial thoughts and ideas, the Foundation assembled a task force of nationally known experts in the fields of manpower training, special education, rehabilitation, marketing, and public relations. Their task was to develop a model comprising the effective features of each field in addressing known problem areas in the employment of people with disabilities. What resulted was the *Bridges . . . from school to work* program.

The *Bridges* program facilitates internships in area businesses for students with disabilities during their senior years in high school. These internships are designed to last at least 2 months and to serve as valuable adjuncts to the students' education. In fact, studies show that young people who obtain paid employment prior to their exit from high school are more likely to be employed as adults (Wagner, 1991).

These internships served three purposes: 1) to provide participating students with up-to-date job training and work experience, 2) to enhance their employment potential as they prepare to exit school, and 3) to provide local employers with a viable source of employees. In fact, participating employers gained critical experience in recruiting, managing, and accommodating employees with disabilities. Figure 4.1 illustrates the *Bridges . . . from school to work* program model.

Developing and implementing this conceptual model required that a local partner with a proven track record be identified. Because of its history of establishing successful partnerships with businesses, TransCen was a primary candidate for the job. However, there are over 70 job placement organizations in the Washington, D.C., metropolitan area—essentially in the backyard of Marriott's corporate headquarters in Bethesda, Maryland; therefore, the Foundation had many options regarding available job placement agencies. It is here that TransCen's previous partnership with Marriott paid off. Although TransCen was well-positioned geographically, it had more importantly established a positive track record with Marriott executives.

One Partnership Becomes the Catalyst for Others

The Foundation's partnership with TransCen led to the establishment of the first *Bridges* site in what was soon to become a national program. By the end of 1993, this partnership had enabled over 500 young people with disabilities to experience paid employment with over 250 Washington, D.C., area companies and organizations. Although employers were not obligated to hire interns permanently, they have extended employment offers to about 70% of the interns to date.

More important is the idea that strong initial partnerships can actually foster multiple partnerships that yield considerable benefits for all involved. With regard to the *Bridges . . . from school to work* program, the initial partnership between TransCen and Marriott became the catalyst for the establishment of partnerships between TransCen and over 250 different employers of varying size over a 4-year period. These employers offered employment opportunities in a significant array of occupational categories, as shown in Table 4.5. These outcomes have elicited the attention of several

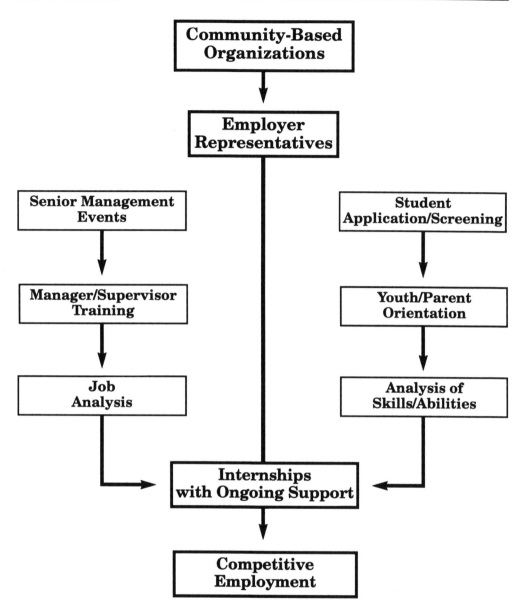

Figure 4.1. The *Bridges . . . from school to work* program model.

important local groups, like the Montgomery County, Maryland, Chamber of Commerce, for instance, which has endorsed and added the *Bridges* program to the program of work for its members. This action quickly allowed *Bridges* to be highly publicized to more than 700 area employers.

As with the previous case studies, it is useful to look at the *Bridges* program in terms of converting features into benefits to gauge respective partners' return on investment. As illustrated in Tables 4.6 and 4.7, the *Bridges* internships provided valuable pregraduation work experience for young people with disabilities as well as low-risk exposure to hiring and managing employees with disabilities for employers.

Table 4.5. Intern placements by occupational category

Occupational category	%
Clerical	32
Food service	11
Customer service	10
Retail	10
Childcare	8
Security	6
Housekeeping	5
Construction	5
Printing	2
Other (includes: microfilm operations, trash removal, car radio installation, landscape labor, warehouse labor, mailroom labor, animal care labor)	11

Outcome Over Process

Marriott's interest in partnering with TransCen entailed considerable expectations. It wasn't sufficient simply to pursue a good cause (i.e., trying to find jobs for young people with disabilities); rather, Marriott fully expected TransCen to develop an internship for every student referred through the *Bridges* program. Therefore, expected outcomes included 100% placement, without exception.

Unfortunately, the statistics are rather disappointing when the employment of people with disabilities is gauged against the public dollars spent on the job placement process. Although very sophisticated processes for preparing people with disabilities for work have been developed (e.g., vocational assessment tools, evaluation methodology, and career counseling), there often is little value placed on the ultimate outcome—jobs. Educators even admit that job placement staff are too often expendable (Schiro-Geist, Walker, & Nerney, 1992). However, the experience with Marriott Foundation ultimately taught that job placement should be the most important activity for any agency. The outcomes thus should have the greatest priority and receive the most attention.

Table 4.6. *Bridges'* features as benefits for employers

Features of *Bridges*	Converted to	Benefits for employers
• Employer representatives		• Single point of contact • Customized consultation on issues involving disability and accommodation • Recruitment assistance • Immediate response and follow up
• Applicant screening		• Pre-screened applicants • Reduced recruitment costs
• Manager training		• Expanded awareness regarding disability • Education in managing a more diverse workforce
• Interns		• Expanded labor pool reflecting a range of talent and diversity • No-risk exposure to training people with disabilities

Table 4.7. Employers' features as benefits for the *Bridges* program

Features of employers	Converted to	Benefits for *Bridges*
• Jobs		• Employment for young people with disabilities
• Business practices		• Modeling effective business practices in day-to-day program operations for maximum efficiency and success
• Resources		• Access to national consultants; in-kind donations; meeting room space; speakers; business advisory members; office furnishings
• Variety of types and sizes of employers		• Wide range of job opportunities in a wide range of occupational categories

PRINCIPLES OF BUSINESS PARTNERSHIPS AT WORK

The challenge is to learn from business and to apply the principles thereby obtained so as to facilitate satisfactory return on investment for all parties. It may be useful to examine how these principles apply to the above case studies.

Developing Mutual Trust

In each case study example, the partnership could not have thrived if not for the strong sense of mutual trust that evolved. In Southland's case, Southland had to trust that TransCen could provide appropriate consultation regarding learning disabilities, thereby enabling Southland's executives to establish and maintain their employee assistance program. Conversely, TransCen trusted that Southland would indeed hire and accommodate young people with learning disabilities.

Similarly, TransCen had to trust that Marriott Corporation would: 1) retain employees with developmental disabilities upon the conclusion of the program, 2) retain its job trainer, and 3) hire more such employees. For its part, Marriott had to trust that TransCen would: 1) subsidize the job trainer, 2) positively represent both the project and Marriott, and 3) follow through on its commitments. The continuation and expansion of the concept and the invitation for TransCen to help develop and pilot the *Bridges* program demonstrate that this trust was rewarded.

As for the *Bridges . . . from school to work* program, the now Director of the Marriott Foundation for People with Disabilities, Mark Donovan, said it best: "It is not a coincidence that a relationship based on trust and good business practices all of a sudden produces all of these spectacular outcomes" (M. Donovan, personal communication, December, 1992).

Adopting Goals and Objectives that Benefit All

Job placement professionals cannot expect employers to provide jobs without first determining their needs. Southland, Marriott, and the variety of employers who participated in the *Bridges* program would have withdrawn from the program were it not for the fact that they also benefitted from the partnerships in significant ways. This is the ultimate in advocacy—forcing businesses to recognize people with disabilities as valuable assets and job placement professionals as credible business partners. Indeed, there is no advantage to adopting a posture that suggests that people with disabilities should be the recipients of businesses' charity.

Forging Long-Term Relationships

It is critical that job placement not be seen simply as "60 days on the job" to facilitate successful closure. The most successful partnerships are those that are viewed by each party as having the potential to endure over the long term. The Southland and Marriott projects continue to produce job opportunities for people with disabilities, thereby helping each corporation to meet its human resource needs. If either of these companies has a problem or question regarding not only an employee hired as the result of the partnerships, but about any issue related to the employment of people with disabilities, they are encouraged to seek guidance from TransCen. Conversely, TransCen can enlist the help of various corporate personnel to obtain information or assistance as needed.

Demanding Mutual Competence

According to Mark Donovan, "What business seeks, first and foremost, from a human service agency is a strong orientation to basic management principles . . . This assures employers ongoing return on investment, upon which business partnerships everywhere are based" (personal communication, December, 1992). Therefore, it is very important that job placement professionals exhibit basic professional competence. Of course, they have every reason to expect the same from any employer with whom they interact.

Adopting a Customer Service Orientation

Every time I called with a question, I got the answer immediately or was given the reason why not. They were always there when I needed them. They checked in on the *Bridges* intern without me having to ask. They always inquired after my needs and those of the company. It was one of the most positive experiences I've had of any kind in terms of service. (S. Hathaway, personal communication, January, 1993)

These words echo those of many employers who hired *Bridges* interns. Indeed, the *Bridges . . . from school to work* program was able to respond to employer demands by developing successful partnerships.

CONCLUSION

As these examples demonstrate, effective partnerships are based on mutual return on investment. When businesses perceive job placement agencies as being capable of delivering valuable commodities—good employees and good services—they are infinitely more willing to enter into partnerships with these agencies, and are therefore more likely to regard them as credible business partners.

REFERENCES

Hawkins, J. (1987). *Follow-up study of special education graduates class of 1985.* Rockville, MD: Montgomery County Public Schools.

Hudson Institute. (1988). *Workforce 2000: Work and workers for the 21st century.* Indianapolis, IN: Author.

Lieberman, G. (1989). Who's making the beds? *Meetings and Conventions, 25*(6), 44–53.

Luecking, R. (1990, November). *Corporate interest in supported employment.* Paper presented at Charting the Course of Quality: A Conference on Supported Employment, Georgia State University, Atlanta.

Luecking, R., & Leedy, M. (1991, January). *Employment and training of persons with disabilities: An implementation guide.* (Available from TransCen, Inc., 451 Hungerford Drive, Rockville, MD 20850).

Luecking, R., Tilson, G., & Wilner, M. (1991). *Corporate employee assistance for workers with learning disabilities.* (Available from TransCen, Inc., 451 Hungerford Drive, Rockville, MD 20850)

Mank, D., Buckley, J., & Rhodes, L. (1990). National issues for implementation of supported employment. In F. Rusch (Ed.), *Supported employment: Models, methods and issues.* Sycamore, IL: Sycamore Press.

Myers, A. (1992, October). *Employer perspectives on supported employment.* Paper presented at the National Symposium on Supported Employment, Virginia Commonwealth University, Norfolk.

Neubert, D., Tilson, G., & Ianacone, R. (1989). Postsecondary transition needs and employment patterns of individuals with mild disabilities. *Exceptional Children, 55,* 494–500.

Nisbet, J., & Hagner, D. (1988). Natural supports in the workplace: A reexamination of supported employment. *Journal of The Association for Persons with Severe Handicaps, 13,* 260–267.

Schiro-Geist, C., Walker, M., & Nerney, N. (1992). Rehabilitation counseling and placement. *American Rehabilitation, 18*(2), 25–27.

Tilson, G., Taymans, J., & Germino-Hausken, E. (1991). *A descriptive study of young adults with mild disabilities who participated in a model postsecondary transition project.* Unpublished manuscript, George Washington University, Department of Teacher Preparation and Special Education, Washington, DC.

Trach, J., & Rusch, F. (1989). Evaluating supported employment programs: The degree of implementation. *Mental Retardation, 94,* 134–139.

TransCen, Inc. (Producer). (1989). *Business sponsored supported employment* (Videotape). Rockville, MD: Producer.

Wagner, M. (1991). *Youth with disabilities: How are they doing? The first comprehensive report from the national longitudinal transition study of special education students* (Contract No. 300-87-0056). Washington, DC: U.S. Department of Education.

JOB DEVELOPMENT AND PLACEMENT— A PRACTICAL FRAMEWORK

Chapter 5 _____

STRUCTURING
THE JOB SEARCH

_____

The foundations must be laid for the job placement process to be a partnership between jobseekers and job placement professionals. Indeed, it is as important to build partnerships with jobseekers as it is to build partnerships with businesses. In fact, the partnerships built with jobseekers become the models for building relationships with employers.

UNDERLYING PRINCIPLES

Effectively structuring the job search requires responsiveness not only to employers, but to jobseekers as well. This responsiveness is predicated on several fundamental principles, each of which is discussed in turn.

Principle #1: Get to know the jobseeker on a personal, rather than evaluative, level. Knowing the jobseeker is the basis for developing an appropriate career management plan. In order to be effective, career management plans must take advantage of individual vocational strengths in a manner consistent with the external demands and realities of the labor market, and should be based on the individual interests, vocational skills, career objectives, and vocational goals of the jobseeker.

Tomeka is a jobseeker enlisting the help of a job placement agency to assist her in finding a job that she likes. Before the initial interview the agency received various medical and psychological reports about her. The medical reports basically discuss her physical limitations, describing in detail the types of impairments she has, her prognoses, and the limitations that she experiences. Psychological evaluations reveal her limited aptitude, give her IQ score, and describe some of the behavioral manifestations of her various problems.

Based on these reports, Tomeka is referred for a vocational evaluation. During the initial meeting, the purpose of the agency is explained, some information about

(continued)

Tomeka's social and educational background is gathered, and her referral is determined to be appropriate.

Tomeka's subsequent vocational evaluation takes 1 week. The vocational evaluation consists of standardized work samples—situational assessments conducted in a vocational evaluation room—and assessment of her work capacity in terms of such factors as attentiveness, ability to stay on-task, and frustration. The evaluation report indicates that Tomeka enjoys clerical work, that her typing speed is 25 words per minute, that her work behaviors indicate a need for prompting [her] to stay on task, and that she seems to be somewhat inattentive in completing assigned tasks. Tomeka is subsequently referred to the local supported employment program for placement (with a job coach) as an entry-level clerical worker.

Tomeka's story represents a typical scenario that may be experienced by jobseekers with disabilities who are referred for job placement services. In order to point out the fact that jobseekers with disabilities frequently encounter a routinized, stereotypical job placement process, details concerning Tomeka's strengths, interests, experiences, and disability were purposely omitted.

Intimately knowing the jobseeker may at first appear to be unnecessary. However, as Tomeka's case study suggests, the information gained through routine diagnostic evaluation is not sufficient to build a partnership or develop a career management plan. Typically, such information serves only to facilitate the delivery of "standardized" services to jobseekers with disabilities.

Too often, little time is spent developing activities aimed at getting to know jobseekers' interests, likes, and strengths. By overlooking this critical step, it becomes difficult to identify vocational strengths and subsequently to empower consumer choice. Thus, successful job placement is jeopardized.

Vocational strengths are predicated upon individual interests and skills. Identification of these interests and skills is necessary in order to facilitate a successful job match. Indeed, the absence of interest leads to job dissatisfaction in much the same way that the absence of skills leads to unsatisfactory job performance.

Principle #2: Developing effective communication is the most basic element in the job placement process. In order to build a relationship with someone, it is essential to listen to and to understand what he or she is communicating. Effective communication entails careful attention to the messages being conveyed as well as expressions of interest on the part of each communicator. Proper communication requires that the listener not interrupt the speaker, not give advice, and not tell the speaker what he or she means. It often requires observing the so-called 75/25 rule: 75% listening and 25% talking.

Listening is an important job placement skill whether one is working with jobseekers, employers, or other community representatives. In fact, when Mark McCormack (1984) was preparing to write his best-selling book on salesmanship, he asked many of his business associates for advice about what to include. Their chief response was: learn to be a good listener.

The skills outlined in Table 5.1 are basic to being a good listener. Good listening skills are essential to developing collaborative relationships with others. They facilitate understanding the individual, developing appropriate career options, and fostering opportunities for choice. They also demonstrate respect for the speaker and ensure that development of a career management plan is predicated upon a collaborative relationship. Relationships are subsequently enhanced by using good listening skills because they facilitate mutual assistance.

Table 5.1. Composite skills of good listening

Skill defined	Useful for
• Paraphrase—summarize the main ideas or thoughts of the speaker	• Indicating that the listener is listening; ensuring accuracy in the communication
• Clarification—check out what is heard in the form of a question and paraphrase	• Checking accuracy of message conveyed; ensuring that words or meanings are not misunderstood
• Reflection—summarize the main affective or emotional feelings of the speaker's message	• Indicating that the listener understands and empathizes with the speaker's feelings
• Exploratory question—ask an open-ended question (e.g., how, what, tell me more)	• Encouraging the speaker to elaborate on the topic; encourages exploration
• Nonverbal attending behavior—body postures and facial expressions that convey interest and empathy	• Indicating interest and attention to the speaker

Good listening skills are essential when dealing with people with disabilities. In these cases, listening and communications skills may be understood and implemented in a broad way, such as observing an individual's reactions to various situations by attending to nonverbal responses. Attending to these nonverbal responses is a means to identifying likes and dislikes. For example, a staff member at TransCen worked with a young woman named Kate with severe mental retardation in order to identify vocational preferences. After visiting several potential jobsites, the staff member reported that she could "see Kate's face light up; her whole body seemed energized" after spending time in the office where she was eventually employed. Indeed, the ability to interpret nonverbal responses is largely dependent on spending sufficient time with the jobseeker and getting to know him or her.

In developing relationships with people with disabilities, it may be necessary to devote a great deal of time engaging in various activities. Spending time with an individual in a variety of settings or conducting different activities while observing the individual's responses are both potential sources of information consistent with assisting that person to identify vocational choices. Responding to nonverbal responses also conveys a respect for the person's determination of choice, even if he or she is unable to communicate that choice directly.

During Tomeka's first interview, it was discovered that she has difficulty in articulating preferences regarding activities or interests. She had limited vocational experience during school and was not exposed to the extracurricular activities that may have served as adequate alternative experience. When asked what she likes to do, she seems to give routine, socially validated responses. However, these are not necessarily representative of her likes and dislikes. Three alternative means that might be helpful in assisting Tomeka to accurately and effectively communicate her likes and dislikes include: spending time with Tomeka at home, visiting various community sites together, and talking to people about their jobs.

Principle #3: Understand barriers to communication and how to avoid them. At times, individuals with limited opportunities or from diverse cultural backgrounds may express interest in career choices that seem either inappropriate or unrealistic. In other cases, jobseekers with disabilities may express little or no interest in a specific vocation. The inability to communicate that frequently exists between a job placement professional and a jobseeker is often erroneously attributed to personal problems of the individual jobseeker. Job placement staff may indicate that a person either has little motivation to work or otherwise expresses little vocational interest. However, it is important to keep in mind that these indications may be the consequence of communication problems as opposed to individual failures.

There are many factors contributing to communication difficulties that may arise when attempting to understand an individual. Among the most significant of these factors are cultural difference and disability biases.

Principle #4: Develop cross-cultural skills to preclude diversity as a barrier to communication.   One barrier interfering with effective communication and the development of partnerships with jobseekers is a lack of cross-cultural awareness. Table 5.2 lists several strategies that may be helpful in this regard.

Culture may be defined as the beliefs and values that operate as explicit and implicit assumptions or guidelines about the way in which people live their lives (Herr & Fabian, 1993). Explicit assumptions include such things as preferred foods, styles of dress, language, hairstyles, customs, and observed holidays. Implicit assumptions comprise things like temporal orientation, values concerning autonomy and independence, and views concerning interpersonal relationships. For example, some Japanese Americans do not value individual achievement and autonomy as highly as do other Americans. Similarly, various ethnic groups differ in terms of their temporal relationships, placing greater emphasis on the past and present than on the future.

An important aspect of listening involves understanding and valuing the cultures of other people. It is important to remember that, as American society becomes increasingly diverse, jobseekers and career management consultants will originate from increasingly divergent ethnic backgrounds. In fact, it is estimated that by the year 2000, over 60% of individuals seeking employment will come from ethnic minorities comprising African and Asian Americans, and Hispanics (Hudson Institute, 1988). Cultural variation will not preclude effective communication unless job placement professionals are naive regarding their assumptions and conceptions about various cultures.

Of course, each of us has developed certain assumptions and biases that may be difficult to articulate because they are embedded in the values with which we were raised—implicit and explicit guidelines as well as religious and social backgrounds of various cultures. These cultural "filters" can subsequently interfere with interpersonal communication and understanding. When we are unaware of our personal assumptions or are unconsciously rejecting the views and beliefs of others' cultures, cultural differences become formidable barriers to communication. Thus, developing cultural competency involves acquiring basic awareness and knowledge concerning cultural differences and the effects that these differences may have on communication.

Culturally competent job placement professionals are not expert regarding cultural diversity, but rather are individuals who have developed good listening skills

Table 5.2. Building cross-cultural competencies for jobseekers

- Assist jobseekers in understanding their cultural backgrounds.
- Discuss cultural differences and their influences on the work world.
- Discuss strategies for dealing with various differences. Define what types of cultural differences are likely to result in misunderstandings.
- Develop strategies that might be useful in interviewing as well as in other job settings.
- Conduct multicultural training and awareness seminars for businesses and employers.

and who are aware of how culture might influence individual perception and communication (McGrath & Axelson, 1993). The skilled job placement professional is aware of and is subsequently willing to accommodate jobseekers' cultural characteristics and value systems, thereby assuming a posture of flexibility and openness. The following box outlines three basic stages for acquiring cultural competence.

---

1. *Awareness.* This stage of developing culturally competent skills is based on "being able to ask the right questions" (Pedersen, 1988, p. 106). Awareness essentially encompasses our attitudes toward people from culturally diverse backgrounds as well as the perceptions, behaviors, and values of others that may differ from our own. One acquires awareness through: 1) talking with different types of people, 2) reading about diverse cultures, 3) examining case studies, and 4) direct contact.

2. *Knowledge.* The second stage discussed in Pedersen (1988) refers to understanding that culture influences individual development. Consequently, job placement professionals need to have some knowledge of the ways in which cultural variables can influence individual attitudes toward work and other vocational activities. Also involved is understanding how different career strategies may elicit different outcomes, depending on the backgrounds and characteristics of individual jobseekers.

3. *Skills.* This final stage refers to acquiring those skills "based both on awareness and on knowledge to bring about appropriate and effective change in multicultural situations" (Pedersen, 1988, p. 107). In other words, this stage involves having sufficient awareness and knowledge to be flexible in trying different approaches for different jobseekers in diverse situations. In this context, multicultural skills may entail understanding the means by which different types of social supports are determined to be effective depending on clients' cultural backgrounds, and subsequently being able to develop effective social supports for individual jobseekers.

Being aware of cultural differences is one way of ensuring that these differences do not become barriers to communication, and thus obstacles to the development of a relationship. However, there are other obstacles to communication that are particularly relevant for people who are working with individuals with disabilities. These obstacles are actually biases regarding ways in which to listen to people with disabilities and the process by which effective methods of intervention are determined.

Principle #5: Be aware of other biases that operate as barriers to good listening.   Three listening biases that job placement professionals need to be aware of are availability, representativeness, and salience. Availability refers to the process by which people with disabilities are routinely limited to certain jobs or services based on available methods and prevailing assumptions rather than on information specific to individuals. Availability impedes the process of communication because the job placement professional is necessarily more intent on satisfying a stereotype rather than focusing on individual understanding. In Tomeka's case study, availability involved: 1) automatic referral for a week-long vocational evaluation, and 2) designing a plan that required supported employment services. Although the plan was not inappropriate for Tomeka, it was predicated on service-available intervention rather than individual skills and interests.

Failure to assess the specific needs of an individual—assuming that he or she is representative of others of the same group—also hinders communication. An example of this is assuming that all jobseekers with mental retardation will have similar vocational interests or will require similar job supports.

When an individual's disability becomes the focal point of an interaction, it may preclude one's ability to communicate with that individual. In other words, emphasizing an individual's disabling condition(s) perpetuates biases regarding disabilities in general. In the case of Tomeka, most of her background reports focused on her impairments, deficits, and needs. Placing emphasis on her skills, interests, and desires requires shifting the focus from the disability to the person.

It is critical to realize that increasing numbers of individuals with disabilities are members of minority groups. This necessitates that culturally competent skills be developed to ensure that the jobseeker is aware of cultural as well as disability biases that might be encountered. Anticipating barriers and prejudices and assisting individual jobseekers to manage them ultimately builds effective coping and self-efficacy skills.

Effective communication skills are fundamental to building partnerships with jobseekers. The purpose of these skills is to become acquainted with the individual and to empower him or her to implement vocational choices. The next step in this fundamental process, then, is assisting the person to identify vocational choices.

Principle #6: A career management approach to job placement involves empowering people to operationalize vocational choices; understanding vocational interests is fundamental to this process. Once a relationship has been established, the first step in developing a career management plan is to identify vocational interests. A person's vocational interests provide a great deal of information about that individual (e.g., the careers that he or she may enjoy, the people that he or she would like to work with, and even the types of work environments that would best meet his or her needs).

Part of the process of adolescent development involves exploring various vocational options through a variety of activities such as: being exposed to people with different jobs, engaging in different roles, reading about occupations, and having opportunities to talk to others. However, for some people, experiences such as these are limited. Economic circumstances, career stereotypes, lack of oppportunity, and cultural differences might all function as barriers to developing vocational preferences. For people with disabilities, these opportunities may even be more severely limited by other factors such as: not having the opportunity to experience a diverse educational environment, being limited to a single classroom, and/or having limited exposure to peers and mentors.

Given these barriers to the exploration process—a process that is critical to identifying vocational interests—effective communication skills and strategies must be implemented for exploring vocational interests.

Principle #7: Use existing techniques for assessing vocational interest cautiously. There are a variety of standardized interest inventories available for measuring patterns of vocational choice. Examples of these inventories include: the Kuder Occupational Information Survey, the Strong Vocational Interest Inventories, the Holland Self Directed Search, and the Myers Briggs Inventory. Although many of these standardized instruments are useful in assisting people to articulate or identify latent vocational interests, they must be administered with caution, especially when dealing with people with disabilities. That is, people with disabilities may not be capable of responding reliably to items that measure interest levels for tasks that they have never encountered. Similarly, many of these standardized tests are based on comparing individual responses to a normative group of respondents. However, this normative group may or may not include people with disabilities. It is therefore important to determine precisely who comprises such a group:

1. Does this group represent an adequate sampling in terms of race, ethnicity, and gender?
2. Does it include people with disabilities?

This kind of information can be obtained from the manuals accompanying the various types of vocational interest inventories.

Although it may not always be wise to use these inventories exclusively in assessing an individual's vocational interests, some may be useful as tools for helping an individual to explore a variety of career options. The results should not be viewed as patterns of definitive occupational interests. However, they can assist in helping the individual to identify and explore a variety of occupational interests.

Principle #8:   Use hands-on methods to explore vocational interests.   Vocational options are best explored through hands-on methods. As stated previously, many young people explore various vocational activities during their adolescent years. Babysitting for neighbors, having a paper route, and participating in various extracurricular activities are all examples of vocational exploration. Similarly, adults considering a career change are often encouraged to conduct information interviews—selecting several vocational options that seem interesting and surveying the businesses, programs, and people who are engaged in those vocations. There is no substitute for this kind of direct, hands-on experience.

For some people with disabilities, opportunities for vocational exploration may be limited. Therefore, it is necessary for job placement professionals to provide such opportunities. Visiting a number of different employment sites such as libraries, offices, health care facilities, and government agencies, and enabling the individual to experience these environments is a good strategy facilitating exposure to the work world. Often, developing internship opportunities during high school is another practical approach to providing hands-on opportunities for vocational exploration.

Developing a plan of action for exploring vocational options is essential. If the jobseeker is unable to conduct these activities alone, the job placement professional should spend time with the jobseeker in order that they may explore various options together.

Principle #9:   Use vocational and other resources to help in the exploration process.   Become familiar with various occupational resource books in order to aid in the vocational exploration process. For example, the *Occupational Outlook Handbook* is a good exploration tool, as are local community guides, the yellow pages and the telephone book, and local places of interest. Indeed, any activity or resource that suggests vocational or occupational choices is appropriate to use. Various computer programs for career exploration are also valuable sources of information. Although these may be costly, jobseekers who are able to use them reap significant benefits. The fact that they facilitate a self-managed and self-directed vocational exploration makes them attractive alternatives for helping jobseekers to explore career options.

Principle #10:   Ensure that jobseekers envision vocational goals.   Developing a vocational goal is predicated on a jobseeker's ability to envision the future—to visualize where he or she would like to be several months or years from now. Vocational development theorists discuss the idea of a career trajectory, a concept that suggests movement into the future. However, it is important to keep in mind that some people, because of experiencial or cultural differences, do not see the importance of this future orientation that is so basic to the career planning process. This may be seen, for example, when a jobseeker seems to be unable to articulate a vocational choice or otherwise resists an entry-level position because he or she does not view the position as a stepping stone to further career development.

The prevailing response to occurrences such as these is to counsel the individual about both the importance of planning and the concepts underlying future promotion and career development. However, if a jobseeker is not thus oriented, it is difficult if not impossible to explain either the process or the importance of planning and goal setting. Unfortunately, it is difficult to develop a partnership that enables that person to set appropriate career goals if he or she is not willing to participate in the planning process. Indeed, fundamental to career management is the ability to visualize a goal and the steps leading to its attainment.

There are several activities that may be useful in initiating intervention that stimulates the development of career goals. Some of these are:

- Invite speakers who have different careers and have explored different options to describe various options and their respective results.
- Initiate lifeline exercises—exercises wherein decisions that were actually made in an individual's life are outlined and their results mapped out.
- Arrange for mentors—people who are established in various occupations and careers—to work with individuals in planning career alternatives.
- Instruct jobseekers to note 10 events—graduating, getting married, getting a new job—and ask them to indicate the ages at which they expect each to occur. Are the ages proximate to the individual's current age? How far into the future has the person planned?

Principle #11: Remember that vocational choice is never related to the type or nature of disability. Decades of research regarding disabilities have demonstrated that levels of severity or impairment are not necessarily related to vocational outcomes. For instance, for people with serious mental illness, psychiatric diagnoses of symptoms are not a predictor of how an individual will function on the job. The development and subsequent success of supported employment programs for people with severe developmental disabilities has adequately demonstrated their ability to work despite their levels of disability. Indeed, an impairment does not necessarily result in lifelong disability. Therefore, job choices must not be circumscribed by predictions regarding future functioning that are based on individual disabilities and deficits.

During her initial meeting with a job placement professional, it is discovered that Natasha has limited information regarding the work world. However, she does indicate that she really enjoys being with other people. It is subsequently noted that she is easy to get along with and that she has a great sense of humor.

Although she has never had a paying job, she was frequently asked by neighbors to babysit when she was in high school. Natasha enjoyed this activity quite a bit. She also helped put together a newsletter for her extracurricular club, Helping Others, during her final 2 academic years.

Based on this information, Natasha and her job coach visited a nursing home, a community theater group, and a newspaper office to explore possible job choices.

CONCLUSION

This chapter sets the stage for the job development and placement process. It outlines those strategies that are frequently overlooked when working with jobseekers with disabilities, but that should comprise the foundation of the job placement process. Fundamental to job placement is knowing jobseekers on a personal level, not simply on the level provided through standardized vocational evaluation tests. This requires both effective communication and the ability to recognize barriers that may preclude the development of a relationship. In addition, job placement requires both attention to various vocational choices and career planning on an individual basis.

REFERENCES

Herr, E.L., & Fabian, E.S. (1993). Curriculum trends in transcultural counseling in counselor education. In J. McFadden (Ed.), *Transcultural counseling: Bilateral and international perspectives* (pp. 305–332). Alexandria, VA: American Association on Counseling and Development.

Hudson Institute. (1988). *Workforce 2000: Work and workers for the 21st century* (Contract No. 3796-RR). Washington, DC: U.S. Government Printing Office.

McCormack, M. (1984). *What they don't teach you at Harvard Business School.* New York: Bantam Books.

McGrath, P., & Avelson, J.A. (1993). *Accessing awareness and developing knowledge: Foundations for skill in a multicultural society.* Belmont, CA: Brooks/Cole Publishing Co.

Pedersen, P. (1988). *A handbook for developing multicultural awareness.* Alexandria, VA: American Association on Counseling and Development.

U.S. Bureau of Labor Statutes. (1988). *Occupational outlook handbook.* Washington, DC: U.S. Department of Labor.

Chapter 6

KNOWING THE CUSTOMER

The most obvious customers for job placement professionals are jobseekers with disabilities. These individuals are also commonly referred to by other terms: clients, recipients, consumers, special education students, and trainees. Traditionally, job placement professionals focus on getting to know particular customers through some type of formal or informal evaluation procedure. However, a marketing management and partnership orientation to job development and placement demands that professionals in this field recognize employers as equally important customers. Although no one would argue that job placement professionals have always interacted with employers, these professionals have not gone far enough to view employers genuinely as customers and to thus treat them accordingly.

WHAT IS A CUSTOMER?

Before looking more closely at specific types of customers, it might prove helpful to provide a definition of the term *customer*. A customer is any person or entity obtaining a service or product from another person or entity. This is usually facilitated through an exchange of money or something of monetary value, or sometimes through a bartering arrangement. Sometimes, goods and services are purchased directly by the customer who will use them; at other times, they are obtained by one customer to be used by another.

Consider a customer in a jewelry store who buys an engagement ring for his girlfriend. The man is clearly the purchaser; yet, the recipient might also be thought of as a customer even though she is not directly responsible for the purchase of the ring. Similarly, consider human services agencies that receive government money to provide services to clients. Despite the fact that the client may not be initially responsible for purchasing the services, he or she is certainly a customer of those services.

In all cases, the customer is a person or entity receiving products or services from another person or entity. Typically, a customer is in the market for a specific commodity when that customer has the desire or need for that commodity.

Getting to Know the Jobseeker

Becoming acquainted with the jobseeker is most often described in terms of vocational evaluation or client assessment. Historically, vocational evaluation has been considered a phase in which a variety of objective and subjective tests or situational assessments are administered to an individual in order to rate his or her vocational skill levels, behaviors, and potential. Vocational evaluation frequently occurs within a limited time frame—at times as little as 2 hours in duration.

When examining the purpose of vocational evaluation, it is helpful to begin with the simple question: "How do people get to know you?" You may respond by saying that people get to know you by spending time with you or by seeing you in a variety of settings. However, it is unlikely that someone could get to know you by seeing you for a short period of time in a setting that generates some anxiety for you so that the behaviors you demonstrate in that setting are atypical or are not necessarily characteristic.

In fact, impressions based on a single encounter often prove inaccurate and are thus modified after later encounters with an individual. For example, how many times have you met someone and developed a first impression that was revised after subsequent meetings? The point here is to illustrate the ways in which people generally get to know one another—through multiple meetings in multiple settings at different times. This is the way that we should become acquainted with people with disabilities, particularly those whose disabilities are significant. Thus, it may become necessary for job placement professionals to re-examine how well present evaluation methods identify a person's likes or capabilities.

Research in social psychology regarding the ways in which individuals with disabilities are evaluated has demonstrated that, when behavior is atypical—when an individual does not conform to pre-established standards—the inclination is to focus on his or her faults or deficits rather than on the environmental context that may be causing such performance. Therefore, it becomes clear that career decisions based on behavior during a brief evaluation—a potentially uncomfortable or unfamiliar situation—is not a valid way of getting to know a jobseeker. The following are several alternative strategies that may be employed in lieu of brief evaluations in order to become familiar with jobseekers.

Strategy #1: Spend Time with Jobseekers A plan of action must be developed for spending time with every jobseeker in a variety of settings, including the local community as well as your office. These meetings should be held in a combination of familiar and unfamiliar locations. Moreover, meeting times should be varied in order to determine whether behaviors are modified at different times of the day.

After each encounter, particularly if the individual's disability is significant, ensure that you are able to identify at least three positive skills demonstrated by the person during that encounter. For instance, if you are accompanying a jobseeker on a vocational exploration activity, be able to list at least three tasks in which the person engaged during the activity (e.g., speaking with another person in the environment, asking questions about the job).

Keep in mind that formal assessment processes, although often yielding good information about an individual, may not accurately represent the person. For every evaluation report, ask yourself, "What do I not know about this person?" Resolve to find answers to this question, and remember to emphasize the person's positive traits.

Strategy #2: Obtain a Wide Range of Information About Jobseekers There are many ways of getting to know people: observing them, reading about them, spending time with them, talking with them, and talking with others who know them. When discussing a person's experiences, solicit as much detail as possible. Try to determine the depth of his or her knowledge, skill levels, strengths, shortcomings, likes and dislikes, and unique familial and cultural traditions. The following list highlights important data to gather about a jobseeker. Ultimately, factors in each of these areas should correspond as closely as possible to the demands posed by targeted jobs and jobsites.

Demographic information
  Name, address, telephone number

Personal information
  Talents
  Skills
  Interests
  Temperament

Vocational information
  Education and training
  Paid work experience
  Volunteer experience
  Social and/or community activities
  Domestic/family activities
  Hobbies or special interests
  Natural abilities and talents
  Needs for accommodation and
    support
  Preferences
  Accomplishments
  Dreams and aspirations

Even seasoned professionals in the disability field can unwittingly overlook the talents and positive attributes of an individual, particularly if he or she has a significant disability. In fact, training in evaluation is often based on the medical model, which emphasizes the identification of deficits and relevant strategies for lessening or alleviating the impact of those deficits.

However, much success has been experienced using a tool developed by Dileo and Langton (1993). They suggest that every professional who represents a jobseeker should be able to conduct what they call a "3–3–3 Assessment." To do this, the job placement professional identifies three concrete skills, three positive personality traits, and three interests or hobbies of the jobseeker. This in turn ensures that the jobseeker's most positive attributes and skills are emphasized.

Although this exercise may seem overly simplistic, it has significant implications. In fact, this basic activity may pose a difficult challenge for professionals representing individuals who face substantial difficulties due to their disabilities, backgrounds, and/or circumstances. It is intended to focus attention on the capabilities and strengths of jobseekers, rather than on their limitations. Indeed, everyone likes to be judged based on their most positive attributes, not on their weaknesses, shortcomings, or failings.

Imagine that you are searching for a job and you are necessarily concerned about making a favorable impression on prospective employers. Part of your job search involves assessment. You are given several pages listing questions such as the following:
  Have you ever

- Been late for an appointment?
- Forgotten an appointment all together?

(continued)

- Yelled at a co-worker?
- Gotten a speeding ticket?
- Called in sick when you really went shopping?

Imagine that a report is made—based on your responses to these questions—that highlights each of your deficits and mistakes. Would you want that report released to prospective employers?

This exaggerated scenario is intended to illustrate what often happens to people with disabilities: their mistakes, weaknesses, limitations, and atypical behaviors are highlighted by reports, while their positive traits are obscured.

If the positive characteristics of a jobseeker with a disability cannot be readily identified, then a professional should not represent that individual to an employer. Indeed, he or she either has little to offer a business, or more likely, the professional is unable to see precisely what the individual does have to offer.

When determining what a jobseeker can offer to an employer, everything possible must be done in order to identify that individual's strengths, talents, interests, and positive personality traits. When faced with the jobseeker's limitations, the professional should ask, "What ideas can this person and I come up with for making accommodations that will help compensate for existing limitations?"

Strategy #3: Identify Barriers to Employment for Jobseekers with Disabilities
Just as important as obtaining a wide range of information about jobseekers is the identification of barriers to employment they may face. People with disabilities are as susceptible to circumstantial obstacles as are people without disabilities. Barriers to employment may be classified into four major categories: voluntary, involuntary, psychological, and situational.

A voluntary obstacle is exemplified by a jobseeker who is unwilling to commute 5 miles to work. In this case, the individual is choosing not to fulfill a required condition of employment. By contrast, an involuntary barrier is something over which the individual has no control, such as the presence of a physical or mental disability or the absence of available public transportation. Psychological barriers occur when an individual assumes that a barrier exists when it in fact does not. Examples of this type of barrier are seen when women are unwilling to accept a position traditionally held by men, or when a person who speaks with an accent refuses a sales position because he or she fears that customers may respond negatively. Finally, situational barriers are those that are inherent to a given situation and are independent of an individual's attitudes or beliefs. Consider the situational barrier for the jobseeker with chronic asthma who applies for a position in a chemical factory.

It is imperative that professionals work with jobseekers to identify existing as well as potential barriers. The professional should be guided by the following questions:

- What is the nature of the barrier (voluntary or involuntary)?
- How could the barrier affect the applicant's job search?
- Is the barrier removable by the jobseeker?
- Is the barrier removable with professional assistance?
- Does barrier removal require outside assistance?
- Is there a way to continue the job search despite the barrier?

A young man named Sam was diagnosed at age 25 as having severe clinical depression. Sam's mental illness was exacerbated by the fact that he had suffered an injury to his spinal cord while in high school, an injury that left his legs paralyzed and therefore necessitated the use of a wheelchair. Prior to becoming physically disabled, Sam possessed impressive skills as a carpenter that he developed while growing up working alongside his father who was a building contractor. He had excelled in his vocational classes and had even received honors for carpentry work done in a small housing development.

Despite his spinal cord injury, Sam was determined to continue carpentry work. Although he was restricted to ground-level tasks, he demonstrated that he was still very capable of utilizing most of his skills.

At that time, Sam was living with his parents in a rural area, and his father drove him to work each day. Unfortunately, soon after Sam graduated from high school, his father died. Because his mother did not drive and Sam did not have a car, a transportation problem immediately arose. Further exacerbating the problem was the fact that there was no available public transportation where the family lived. One of Sam's friends offered to take him to work for several weeks, but the 50-mile trek ultimately proved to be too much for the friend and he was forced to stop driving Sam to work each day.

Sam subsequently became despondent and quit his job. His mother became concerned about his mental state and took him to see a psychologist. The psychologist suggested that Sam was showing definite signs of serious depression and recommended counseling. Sam's mother was opposed to counseling, saying that Sam should just "get his act together." The situation deteriorated to the point where Sam refused to get out of bed in the morning.

By the time a job placement professional met Sam, it was obvious that there were a number of significant barriers to employment. These barriers fell into four categories: voluntary, involuntary, psychological, and situational. The first step, therefore, was to work closely with Sam to clearly identify individual barriers and to devise an appropriate plan of action for addressing each.

Too often, job placement professionals under considerable pressure to make a placement may fail to identify all barriers that will seriously affect a jobseeker's ability to obtain and maintain satisfactory employment. However, the importance of identifying each of these barriers cannot be stressed enough.

Strategy #4: Identify Potential Accommodations   The hard work has only just begun as a job placement professional becomes acquainted with a jobseeker's interests, skills, aspirations, personality, experiences, limitations, and barriers. An error frequently made by professionals is to believe that, despite the fact that a jobseeker possesses some positive attributes that would benefit an employer, certain barriers (e.g., environmental or physical limitations) will ultimately preclude employment or severely limit employment options. It is a serious mistake for job placement professionals to determine a jobseeker's employability without carefully considering ways in which a potential barrier may be alleviated or mitigated through some type of accommodation.

Accommodation is defined by the U.S. Equal Employment Opportunity Commission as any change in the work environment or in the way things are usually done that enables a qualified individual with a disability to have equal access to employment opportunities and to perform a job to the best of his or her ability (Pimental, Baker, & Tilson, 1991). Job placement professionals must develop a much broader perspective regarding accommodation. Indeed, accommodations should be viewed as actions taken to address identified barriers faced by jobseekers.

The concept of accommodations and their provision is not limited to people with disabilities. In each of our lives, accommodations are required to solve or respond to the many challenges that confront us each day.

A simple, problem-solving approach to identifying barriers and providing appropriate accommodations for jobseekers or employees with disabilities is that for which job placement professionals should strive. What is the specific barrier? What can be done about it? How can accommodation be facilitated? What resources can be used? This process should be an integral part of becoming acquainted with jobseekers. However, accommodations should be considered from the first meeting between the professional and the jobseeker. Indeed, accommodations should be provided before the jobseeker starts his or her job. Three categories of accommodation are outlined below.

In simplest terms, accommodations are actions taken that alleviate, compensate for, or mitigate a barrier faced by a jobseeker or an employee with a disability. Furthermore, appropriate and successful accommodations actually capitalize on and maximize an individual's positive attributes.

Accommodations can be described as falling into three major categories:

1. Physical accommodations: providing special equipment or modifying existing equipment or facilities, as needed.
2. Changes in how things are done: for example, reading an employment test to an applicant who has mental retardation and who is thus unable to read the test himself.
3. Services and resources: for example, an interpreter for a jobseeker who is deaf, schedule changes for a person with mental illness, or substance abuse treatment programs for people who are addicts.

A job placement professional's attention needs to remain solely on individual jobseekers, not on their disabilities. From the initial meetings with jobseekers, the professional should be working with them to identify and test potential accommodation strategies. This in turn invites creative problem solving that can substantially augment options and opportunities for individuals.

Consider the case of Julius, a 50-year-old man with cerebral palsy. Since childhood, he has used a manual wheelchair that he guides with his feet. When first meeting him, one is struck by a number of things: the constant motion of his entire body due to extensive uncontrollable muscle spasms, his disheveled clothing that is frequently stained with food or liquid, the sounds he makes (his speech is virtually unintelligible), and the manner in which he struggles to eat. However, one is also struck by his twinkling blue eyes that respond instantly to anyone who takes a moment to interact with him as well as by his eagerness to display a worn three-ring binder with laminated pages of phrases and letters—his low-tech communication system.

Clearly, if one were to focus solely on Julius's disability, he seems to have a significant impairment. However, suppose you were in a position to represent him as a jobseeker. In getting to know Julius, you would need to look beyond his disability in realizing his abilities. You would need to find out, for instance, that Julius loves to joke

(continued)

around—to tease and to be teased. His record and compact disc collection is impressive, comprised primarily of opera and big band music. Writing poetry has been a hobby since he was a child, and it reflects deep thought and talent for verbal description. In fact, during the last few years, Julius has written several articles about his experiences as a citizen with a disability. These articles are well-constructed, informative, moving, and even humorous. He slowly creates these pieces on his computer at home, and he has even expressed interest in approaching a publisher about some of his work.

At home, Julius's level of independence is astonishing. He has somehow devised ways by which to care for himself, with only 4 hours of outside assistance per day. He bathes, gets into and out of bed, dresses, and even cooks (frozen microwavable meals). Indeed, in all that he does, he has demonstrated his tenacity and determination.

Based on this very brief profile, one should be able to ascertain the positive qualities and marketable talents that Julius possesses. It is true that his disability is significant. However, it is equally true that he has identified and effectively used accommodations that have helped him to utilize his talents. Imagine the potential accommodations and possibilities for Julius that have not yet been explored.

Julius's story points to the importance of addressing jobseekers' needs by drawing attention to specific solutions and accommodations to various potential barriers. Furthermore, it illustrates that options and possibilities are truly feasible when a responsive orientation is utilized.

Strategy #5: Be Responsive Responsiveness first requires listening—a skill reviewed in previous chapters. For job placement professionals, this necessitates that every effort be made to solicit ideas from jobseekers. They should be encouraged to develop confidence in their abilities to advocate for and help themselves. This does not entail less work for professionals; contrarily, it holds professionals more accountable for determining the precise type(s) of support to provide for each individual. Just as an engineer with one division of General Electric may have to use one approach with parts supplier B and another with parts supplier A, the job placement professional must constantly adjust his or her methods to suit individual jobseekers with disabilities.

Essentially, effective partnerships are predicated upon becoming acquainted with jobseekers. Ignoring this, or relying on evaluation reports whose focus is on deficits rather than strengths and skills, impairs this partnership process.

Getting to Know the Employer

Traditionally, job placement professionals have approached employers with both trepidation and awe. They have tended to view the business community as an entity to be reckoned with rather than as a viable business partner. This may be the result of a "hire the handicapped" orientation—an orientation implying that employers should hire jobseekers with disabilities as a gesture of good will. Human services workers, influenced by this orientation, often tend to devote their attention primarily to the needs of jobseekers, thereby approaching employers for only one reason: to secure jobs.

Unfortunately, viewing employers as adversaries or philanthropists rather than as partners tends to be counterproductive. Doesn't it make sense that employers also have needs, expectations, and concerns that must be addressed? Isn't it critical to bear in mind the reasons that companies exist in the first place, and why they hire the people they hire?

Businesses are in business to do business. They produce goods and services to: 1) make a profit (if they are a private corporation), 2) address a specific societal issue (if they are a nonprofit organization), or 3) serve the public (if they are a government agency or body of elected officials). Regardless of the type of business, each has customers—people or entities who will conceivably benefit from available goods and/or services.

Can a business also be a customer? Of course it can. Consider a large corporation like the Ford Motor Company. Think of the hundreds of companies that supply materials and technical expertise to that one corporate entity. Even nonprofit organizations and government agencies may be considered customers when they receive services and materials from outside sources or contractors.

When a business utilizes the services of a job placement agency, that business becomes a customer. The following strategies are intended to aid job placement professionals in viewing businesses as valuable customers. The reader will note that, as in other sections of this book, the terms *employer*, *business*, and *company* are used interchangeably.

Strategy #1: Become Knowledgeable About the Business World An important first step toward getting to know employers as customers is to appreciate the fact that businesses are in business to do business. For job placement professionals, this notion should underlie every interaction with employers. Employers hire people who will produce desired outcomes following precise specifications guided by established standards. They do not hire people if these things will be jeopardized. It is not only the economic giants who are guided by this principle. In fact, all employers, including human services organizations, make every effort to employ only those people who will assist them in meeting their goals.

Become an ardent student of employers in your community. Take a close look at the *Yellow Pages* to get an idea of the range and scope of American business. Make it your mission to learn, in every way possible, about each of the various industries and companies that exist. Business magazines, trade journals, and local and/or state business newspapers are excellent sources of information regarding opportunities, trends, and projections. Ensure that you familiarize yourself with each type of business—large corporations, small businesses, nonprofit organizations, and government agencies.

In addition, arrange on-site visits to businesses, agencies, and government offices. Talk with friends and relatives about where they work and what they do. Talk with people at community events and attend local business meetings like those at your local Chambers of Commerce. You probably will not get specific job leads from these activities, but you will develop both an information base and a potential network of people that will eventually facilitate jobs.

Strategy #2: Distinguish Between the "Employer as Individual" and the "Employer as Organization" Be specific in identifying what is meant by employer. It can refer to an entire company (i.e., IBM is an employer, as are the U.S. Department of Defense and the U.S. Congress), or it can refer to any person within that company (e.g., personnel specialist, foreman, direct supervisor, human resource director, CEO, and/or line worker).

It is critical that job placement professionals make this distinction between employers as organizations and employers as individuals because two levels of job development necessarily occur: the first, as stated above, is to become familiar with industries within the community and companies within each industry; the second level is the "people" level—the level at which interactions occur that lead to jobs.

Consider a single position within a given company, for example, a bakery supervisor. This individual has a business identity with a specific title and a defined role. However, a bakery supervisor in a store that is part of a larger grocery chain may have a role different from that of someone with the same title who works for a small family-owned bakery shop. It is important that job placement professionals be aware of this fact when interacting with each of these employers.

It is of primary importance to remember that each bakery supervisor is in fact a human being who is affected by the things that affect us all. Indeed, either person may be a parent, a former truck driver, a person with a history of illness, a non–English-speaking immigrant, or an elderly woman or man. This may seem like a ridiculously obvious statement, but it is often the most obvious things that are overlooked. Becoming acquainted with an employer entails getting to know the people who perform employer roles. It is ironic that many job placement professionals frequently dislike the task of job development. However, these same people, when asked why they chose human services as a career, will say that they enjoy working with people.

Strategy #3: *Know Your Services and Their Benefits for Employers* Become extremely familiar with the features of your program and its services prior to making initial contacts with employers. When these first contacts are made, ask questions to determine what businesspeople perceive as their companies' needs; listen rather than talk.

Ensure that you are able to articulate how the features of your services can benefit the companies with which you would like to conduct business. Customers like to be given choices. Thus, be prepared with a menu of options as well as a list of potential job applicants. For instance, perhaps an employer is interested in obtaining technical assistance regarding the issue of reasonable accommodation. Who in your agency can provide that service? What about disability awareness training? What if that employer is experiencing difficulties in developing supervisors' capacity to work with people with disabilities? How can you help in these cases?

It is much easier to reach an agreement with an employer when you are able to provide him or her with several options from which to choose. One employer may claim that he or she does not need to hire anyone and therefore does not require assistance in job analysis, but could nonetheless use basic introductory training on disability issues. Providing this service will necessarily make this employer a customer of your agency.

Strategy #4: *Recognize Multiple Contact Sources and Join Business Organizations* Common questions posed by novice job placement professionals include: "Where do I begin to make contacts?" or "Where do I find job leads?" Some inexperienced professionals may be fortunate enough to be joining an agency that is well-known in the community and thus has already developed an extensive network of employer contacts. For this professional, in addition to meeting existing contacts, the goal will be to expand the network. However, if an agency has few business contacts, it may be necessary for an incoming professional to start from scratch. The following are a few suggestions for doing just that:

- Join Chambers of Commerce and other businesses and civic groups where businesspeople associate; become involved in various activities sponsored by these organizations.

- Ask colleagues, friends, and relatives for the names and telephone numbers of any people they may know in the working world; ask local merchants, doctors, dentists, and/or lawyers to do the same.
- Ask employers with whom you already have a good working relationship to introduce you to colleagues within their companies and to give you the names and numbers of suppliers and vendors with whom their companies do business.
- If your agency has a business or other advisory board, inquire about becoming active with that group.
- Be alert to the possibility of making valuable employer contacts when you least expect to, for example, during an off-hours recreational activity.
- Peruse classified ads regularly and cultivate contacts for later follow up; do not limit use of classifieds to job leads only.

Questions subsequently arise regarding the reasons for making business contacts in the first place. The most salient reasons are:

- Job placement agencies have both an interest and a stake in the economic vitality of their communities.
- An agency's budget may make it a viable force in a community's economy. For example, TransCen has a budget of $1.5 million and a staff of 35. It thus contributes significantly to the local workforce and local revenue.
- They allow you to learn from businesses—what works and what doesn't, as well as tips and techniques. Essentially, they provide a "laboratory" for partnerships.
- They facilitate networking opportunities.
- They allow you to become acquainted with the economic issues of the community.

A note of advice: join organizations with a genuine intention of becoming contributors. Participate in committees and volunteer for assignments. Be perceived as a "helping hand." You will be taken more seriously and your networking will pay off in ways that you do not anticipate. Indeed, it is amazing to realize how quickly cold contacts can become familiar partners.

The Center for Work, Inc., developed an excellent reputation for quality service provision in the small community in which it was located. The organization, which was devoted to providing competitive employment opportunities for people with disabilities, was noted for its responsiveness, its follow through, its understanding of employers' needs, and its ability to adapt services to identifiable labor market demands. In order to expand the potential pool of employers seeking its services, the Center took steps to expand its market base in a manner that fostered employer contacts. It became active in the local Chamber of Commerce, made speeches and presentations regarding disability issues, conducted seminars about the ADA, and wrote letters to the editors of local newspapers. Because of these activities, the Center noted that, in 1 year, the number of initial contacts resulting in positive service outcomes (i.e., assisting people with disabilities to get or keep jobs) increased by over 50%. In fact, relevant statistics suggest that, of the successful professional human services organizations (i.e., those earning over $100,000 per year), over 70% employ a variety of networking activities similar to those listed above.

Strategy #5: Let Employers Know Why You Are Contacting Them   After identifying a potential employer contact, the job placement professional must then decide how and when to next get in touch with that person. Businesspeople—particularly those involved in the areas of human resources, personnel, and management—are bombarded regularly by potential contacts, both from within and outside their companies. Your time as well as that of the people you are contacting is very valuable. When initiating contact—calling, writing, or visiting—clearly state your purpose. Always ask whether this is a convenient time and suggest an alternative time if it is not. When you do make contact, be concise and direct. Use as little time as necessary to make your points. Impress your contact by taking only 15 minutes when she is expecting 30.

Strategy #6: *Know the Decision-Making Process for Hiring* Assuming that your primary task is helping jobseekers to identify job leads and subsequently to go through the application and interviewing process, a logical question concerns who has the authority to hire within a targeted company. Is there only one person in an organization who is responsible for hiring? How easy will it be to gain access to this decision maker?

There are several basic issues that must be considered with regard to the hiring process:

- The company's need to hire
- How applicants are typically recruited
- The criteria by which the applicants will be screened and interviewed
- The final hiring decision
- The time frame in which the hiring decision must be made

Depending on the size of the company, any number of people may be charged with resolving these issues. In fact, as new decisions are made, the process itself may change. It is misleading and overly simplistic to think in terms of one person being the only decision maker unless the particular company is very small and its owner makes all the decisions. This may seem complex, but the benefit is that anyone you contact may be in some way involved with the hiring process. The following list presents several scenarios in which this is the case.

- Through frequent visits to a local auto repair shop, you have gotten to know most of the workers. You've chatted with them and they've seen you with different jobseekers. One of the workers will soon be moving to another town. He is loyal to the shop and therefore wants to find a good replacement. He contacts you for ideas.
- Victor works for a well-known restaurant chain. He recently attended one of your agency's seminars on the ADA. You have had a number of interactions with Victor and have thus established a good rapport. One day, Victor finds a letter of resignation from one of his banquet servers. Faced with a big event in 2 weeks, he is anxious to hire a new server. He calls you and asks, "Do you happen to have any folks who'd be interested in this job?"
- A long-time friend of yours is the personnel manager for a bank. Through the grapevine, he hears about a pending opening for a teller position. Remembering his last contact with you at a Chamber of Commerce mixer, he gives you a call prior to advertising the position.
- You read in your local community newspaper about a company that is expanding its operations. You call a friend of a friend who works for this company and she tells you who will be in charge of hiring during the expansion.
- The brother of a friend of yours has worked for a particular company for several

---

(continued)

years. Although his job has nothing to do with personnel, management, or hiring, he is a highly respected employee whose opinion is highly regarded by management. Whenever there is a job opening in his area, management asks this man for his recommendations.

The next step—finding out who makes the final decisions regarding hiring—can be difficult and should be handled as diplomatically as possible. Therefore, it is wise to obtain information like the following from a contact person with whom you already have developed a good rapport:

- Is there one particular person who makes the final decisions regarding hiring?
- Does this person do the hiring for all departments?
- Are supervisors involved in making these decisions?
- How does the company select candidates to be interviewed?
- How does the company recruit new applicants?
- How does the company decide what the minimum qualifications are for a position?

Essentially, you are trying to discover the idiosyncracies of a company's hiring process. However, do not solicit answers to these questions from a cold contact—someone you have not met or talked with before. It is wise to develop a basic working relationship with a company representative first.

Strategy # 7: Stay in Touch with Contacts Establish ongoing relationships with contacts. Utilize any medium of communication available to you—mail, visits, and phone (or "MVP" as Dileo & Langton [1993] call it)—to remain in contact on a regular basis.

A very basic yet effective tack is to ask how things are going for them. Remind them that you are available to assist them at any time. Remember that maintaining contact facilitates long-term relationships. Move away from the tendency to contact an employer only when you are searching for a job for a jobseeker. In the long run, more jobs will be secured as a result of trusting relationships that are maintained over time.

Strategy #8: Analyze All Aspects of Targeted Jobs After becoming acquainted with an employer, specific jobs should be targeted for specific jobseekers with whom you are working. Analyze each job carefully. Investigate essential job tasks; required skills and credentials, the physical environment, predominant regulations, policies, and procedures; and the level of interaction among co-workers and supervisors. Also, analyze the employment process: recruitment, hiring, training, promotion, evaluation, and supervision.

Because these issues may or may not be addressed in a standard job analysis form, assume responsibility for gathering relevant data on your own. This can be done by interviewing company personnel, observing other personnel, meeting with company supervisors, and researching targeted positions.

CONCLUSION

Knowing the customer is critical for job placement personnel. Indeed, both jobseekers and employers are identified as customers of job placement professionals. Before services or products (i.e., commodities) can be delivered to any customer, it is imperative that the person or entity providing those commodities learns as much as possible about that customer's desires, needs, and expectations. The ideal way to learn about customers or potential customers is to listen closely to them and establish a rapport. Building rapport takes time, enthusiasm, consistency, and genuineness, and necessarily presumes that each party has something to offer the others. With such customer-oriented attributes, the job placement professional will experience a much higher level of success.

REFERENCES

Dileo, D., & Langton, D. (1993). *Get the marketing edge! A job developer's toolkit for people with disabilities.* St. Augustine, FL: Training Resource Network.

McCormack, M. (1984). *What they don't teach you at Harvard Business School.* New York: Bantam Books.

Pimental, R., Baker, L., & Tilson, G. (1991, April). *The Americans with Disabilities Act: Making the ADA work for you.* (Available from Milt Wright & Associates, Inc., 19141 Parthenia St., Suite 3, Northridge, CA 91324)

Chapter 7 ————————————————

MARKETING TO
PROSPECTIVE EMPLOYERS

——

When a company has a commodity (i.e., products and/or services) to sell, it typically advertises its features, its cost, and its availability, as well as ways that it may be obtained by customers. If prospective customers have no idea that the commodity exists, it may just as well be nonexistent. Indeed, it does not find a market; hence, there is no customer.

In 1989, the Marriott Foundation for People with Disabilities conducted an informal, national poll of representatives from many different corporations. When asked, "Is your company interested in recruiting and hiring more people with disabilities?", most representatives responded affirmatively. A follow-up question asked, "What barriers may have prevented, or are preventing, your company from successfully recruiting and hiring qualified people with disabilities?" After expecting to hear a litany of comments like "people with disabilities cannot work," "accommodations are burdensome and prohibitively expensive," or "insurance rates will go up," the Foundation's staff was astounded to hear the actual responses. Company representatives reported that they were unsuccessful in recruiting and employing people with disabilities because they did not know where to find qualified applicants. Incredulous, the interviewers asked an impromptu follow up: "Where do you think you would find these applicants?" "The yellow pages" was suggested by a number of key respondents.

On one level, this is an amusing response. It conjures images of personnel specialists "letting their fingers do the walking" ("Do I look under 'D' for disability or what?"). On a more serious note, the responses to this question point to a significant problem for both jobseekers with disabilities and the professionals who represent them: the business community is, for the most part, unaware of job placement services. Jobseekers with disabilities are unable to let employers know that they are available, job placement professionals are not establishing enough contacts in the business community, and service agencies are not doing effective public relations work. Clearly, there is a substantial need on the part of job placement agencies to develop and implement marketing strategies.

MARKETING IS REACTIVE AND PROACTIVE

Products and services are developed and made available because their producer has [supposedly] determined a need. In this sense, the producer reacts to that specific need. However, highly effective producers know the value both of anticipating needs for goods and services and of constantly improving goods and services that already exist.

In either case, effective marketing involves three critical components: 1) knowing the customer, 2) knowing products and services thoroughly, and 3) advertising the availability of products and services. Effective marketing in for-profit businesses and not-for-profit agencies necessarily involves each of these components. The reader is encouraged to reflect on the degree to which these critical elements are included in his or her current job placement efforts.

Know Your Products and Services

Chapter 6 is devoted to becoming acquainted with the customer. The next critical step is to become extremely familiar with the goods and services you or your agency is making available to customers, both present and prospective. Most job placement professionals would claim that they are familiar with the services they are delivering. However, far too many of these professionals are unable to describe adequately and succinctly (particularly to employers) what it is they are offering. For example, they are not able to respond succinctly to the simple question, "What does your agency do?" This may be the result of having not listened to prospective customers to ascertain their needs or of neglecting to articulate features as benefits designed to address those needs. In both cases, the professional fails to capitalize on the features-to-benefits concept. Therefore, marketing efforts are hampered; they do not result in desired outcomes for jobseekers with disabilities.

Inform Employers of Available Services

Failure to inform employers that a job placement agency exists and that its services represent a valuable potential resource is a costly mistake that occurs too frequently. Consider this scenario: you get a craving for a hamburger, but you are unaware that a new fast food restaurant has just opened close to your home. Because you do not want to drive across town, you decide to do without the hamburger. Consequently, the new restaurant loses a prospective customer because it failed to advertise.

Employers are frequently unaware of agencies representing jobseekers with disabilities that exist in their communities. Informing prospective employers of available services is, therefore, a fundamental responsibility of job placement professionals. The following are some specific strategies for achieving this basic marketing goal.

Strategy #1:   Know What Employers Want and Expect   In conducting their marketing efforts, job placement professionals should keep in mind that most employers want and expect a variety of services and products: good workers, efficiency, convenience, acceptable costs, choice, quick problem solving, quality, flexibility, and technical assistance in resolving specific problems or issues. In addition to these standard expectations, some employers may have unique needs that must be considered as well (e.g., specific employee skill requirements).

In order to determine what employers want and expect, job placement professionals must be prepared to gather information from a variety of sources, including face-to-face discussion, careful observation during on-site visits, and even articles in the business sections of local newspapers. For instance, after reading an article about a local electronics firm facing the challenge of accommodating increased numbers of applicants who did not speak English, a job placement professional came up with a list of ideas of ways in which to assist the company, especially with regard to accommodating workers with disabilities. She subsequently presented her services to that company, thereby responding to their needs as well as those of the jobseekers with disabilities she represented.

By knowing what employers want and expect, job placement professionals can offer services that will capture the attention of prospective employers and that will subsequently benefit those employers who choose to become customers.

Strategy #2: Know Available Services and Programs What is the "package of services" that will be provided to customers? No marketing plan can be developed until you are familiar with the product being sold. If job placement professionals find themselves representing services that are not specifically defined by the agency with whom they are associated, it is imperative that these professionals work with colleagues in their agencies to compose a succinct mission statement that includes specific and measurable service features.

As an example of how important it is for job placement professionals to know the services they offer, consider the products and services provided by the following business entities:

- A real estate agency
- A large kitchen appliance department in a widely known department store
- The local public high school
- An auto repair shop
- A hotel catering department

In each of these businesses, we can identify the ranges and types of products and services that are produced and provided, respectively. In order to be successful, the representatives of these organizations must have a solid understanding of the specific commodities being marketed and must be able to adequately present their features to prospective customers. Once prospective customers decide that specific commodities meet their needs, a sale is made.

The following exercise may be helpful in training job placement professionals. It illustrates the importance not only of knowing the services and resources provided by an agency, but also of being able to catch the attention of prospective employers quickly. Job placement professionals are asked to imagine entering an elevator with one other person. While riding from the 15th floor to the lobby, the other passenger initiates a casual conversation: "I noticed you work for FYI Placement Services. What does your company do?" Because there isn't time to launch into a long explanation, the point is to respond with something that catches the person's attention. For exam-

(continued)

ple: "We're an organization that provides resources and consultation services to companies that hire people with disabilities." The professional's goal here is to emphasize the services available to employers. The job placement professional is then in a perfect position to exchange business cards with the fellow passenger and to follow up at a later time.

The elevator setting is merely one example; there are in fact numerous situations where job placement professionals may have brief, spontaneous interactions with various company representatives.

Strategy #3: Study the Local Business Community It is very important that job placement professionals become familiar with their local business communities. Knowing which industries exist and how they operate is critical. The professional should strive to become a consumer of business news in order to remain abreast of and subsequently to respond to current issues and trends. Furthermore, this research can help you to become more savvy when communicating with businesspeople, thus enhancing your credibility.

Strategy #4: Develop and Use Promotional Marketing Materials Develop promotional marketing materials that illustrate for employers the scope of available services. All materials should be professional and should avoid human services jargon, such as descriptions of supported employment in work adjustment training.

Look at promotional materials from other companies and organizations to develop ideas. Then, draft your materials and solicit feedback from businesspeople in your community. If the agency's budget severely constrains the extent to which you can develop marketing materials (i.e., brochures), at least prepare a succinct, well-edited information sheet printed on high-quality paper.

Remember, you represent your agency in much the same way that employers represent their businesses. Therefore, all of your materials should be business-like and professional.

Strategy #5: Consider Your Business Card a Marketing Tool The business card is considered a standard item for most businesspeople. It is easily distributed and is relatively inexpensive to produce. Most importantly, it provides your contacts with basic information that they need about you: your name, your company affiliation, perhaps your position, your address and telephone number, and, on many effective cards, the nature of the organization that you represent.

Surprisingly, there are many job placement professionals who do not have or use business cards. This is a significant oversight. Any professional whose goal is to become known in the business community should take full advantage of this tool.

Just as good conversation is characterized by interactive dialogue, an exchange of business cards is a gesture of communication. There are many occasions, both formal and informal, when business cards can be distributed to potential contacts. One technique that is often effective is to write a brief note on your business card to remind its recipient of your initial interaction. This notation may subsequently jog the recipient's memory so that he or she remembers specifically why he or she should contact you. Similarly, you may write a notation on a business card that you have received reminding you of when and why you should re-establish contact: "Met 6/23/93 at Chamber Breakfast; interested in ADA training; has contacts for job leads in clerical positions."

Strategy #6: Conduct Marketing Presentations Develop and conduct seminars or similar special events to which you invite targeted company representatives to learn about available services. These seminars should be timely and informative as well as interesting. For example, a seminar on reasonable accommodation or the ADA may attract many participants. Invite effective speakers who will cover relevant topics. Partnerships with respected businesses or business organizations in this regard may bolster credibility as well.

Strategy #7:   Market Services, Not Disabilities   Avoid "selling" people with disabilities. You are essentially a disabilities issues consultant as well as an employer resource. Keep in mind that your primary intention when presenting a candidate for employment is to help him or her to market those attributes and talents that the employer is seeking. Think in terms of what you are actually offering the employer: a prescreened applicant, assistance with workplace accommodations, and consultation for ongoing employment issues and concerns.

Strategy #8:   Use Past Partners as References   Contact people with whom you have had successful partnerships in the past and ask them to provide references for your newer contacts. Conversely, inform new contacts of companies with which you have worked successfully, referring them to representatives from those companies who will endorse your service program. Indeed, sincere testimonials can have a great impact.

Strategy #9:   Turn Contacts Into Prospects, Prospects Into Customers   Effective job development and placement requires that a large customer base be established, one ideally comprising happy customers. Indeed, satisfied customers are repeat customers, and they often help to market your services to others (Levinson, 1989). After all, the job placement professional's goal is to make as many people aware of available services as possible, thereby making contacts and soliciting potential prospects.

Prospects are contacts who are aware of your services and have expressed an interest in availing themselves of those services. Once initial contacts are turned into prospects, you have begun establishing successful business partnerships. Nurture these professional friendships and you will ultimately establish a strong customer base.

Strategy #10:   Continually Make New Contacts   Although some job placement professionals actually thrive on making new contacts, many despise the task. Cold calling may be particularly daunting if your purpose is solely to establish a placement for a jobseeker. However, if you use a marketing approach that focuses on employers' needs and the range of available services, the pressure of initial calls may be significantly alleviated.

Denise Bissonnette, a partner and trainer with Milt Wright and Associates, tells her job placement trainees: "When an employer tells you there are no openings, the only thing you hear is no. Listen to the employer. What he or she is saying is *not at the present time*" (D. Bissonnette, personal communication, November, 1992). Denise also points out that job placement is a numbers game; indeed, it takes many contacts to gain a bona fide customer.

Consider this situation: a job placement professional representing an agency contacts a personnel manager on Monday morning to find out if there are any openings in her company. The manager informs the job placement professional that there are no openings. The next day, that personnel manager runs into a supervisor who mentions that he will be losing an employee and will be looking for a replacement. That afternoon, a job developer from another agency contacts the manager, who now says,

(continued)

"As a matter of fact, we do have an opening." Thus, both timing and luck played a part in this successful outcome.

Now consider a different scenario: a job placement professional from an agency contacts a company's personnel manager on Monday. She informs the manager of her agency's existence and the range of services that it can provide to the manager's company. The job placement professional also asks key questions about the company; she learns that there are no openings at the present time. Nevertheless, she tells the manager that she will forward materials outlining available services. The exchange ends positively. The next morning, the manager sees a supervisor who mentions that one of his workers is leaving and that a replacement would be needed. As the manager returns to his office, he remembers the job placement professional because of the friendly rapport that she established with him; he decides to give her a call.

Again, many contacts are necessary in order to establish a strong customer base. Time must therefore be allocated to facilitate effective public relations.

Strategy #11: Build Business Friendships Take advantage of every opportunity to network—to make employers aware of yourself and the agency that you represent. Although jobs may not be available at the present time, you want employers to think of you and the agency that you represent when job openings do come up. In the meantime, suggest other ways in which you may be of service to employer contacts. If employer contacts come to know and respect you, they will be more likely to contact you when a situation necessitating job placement services arises. This may be referred to as the "top of mind" concept.

When you hear the slogan, "Uh-Huh," you think Diet Pepsi. When you think of photocopy machines, your first thought is Xerox. When someone says computer, you immediately think IBM or Apple. When you sneeze, you reach for a Kleenex.

These companies have made a concerted effort to make their products and services well-known to their customers. They have done this by providing quality products and services consistently on demand. This is the top of mind concept.

A major goal of job placement professionals should be to capitalize on the top of mind concept. When employers have available job opportunities, you want them to think of you and your agency's services. When an employer is concerned that there is a person with a disability in the accounting department who requires accommodation, you want that employer to contact you for assistance. This is done by building strong relationships with employers, by providing excellent services, and by establishing a posture of high visibility in the local community.

Strategy #12: Use Business Letters as an Effective Public Relations Tool Professionals should get into the habit of sending many individualized letters to employers: 1) as cover letters for marketing materials, 2) to thank contacts for their time, and 3) to reiterate in writing an exchange that may have taken place verbally.

Succinct business letters sent in conjunction with promotional materials to targeted employers are a good way to establish professional contacts. Therein mention that you will follow up with a telephone call 1 week later. The correspondence is thus analogous to cold calling.

Business letters used in combination with face-to-face meetings and telephone conversations can be extremely influential to prospective customers. Just as negative impressions are made by a person with poor hygiene, a carelessly written business letter will leave its recipient with a bad impression of the professional who sent it and the agency that he or she represents. In this event, there is even a possibility that the contact person will be misled into thinking that people with disabilities are not desirable employees.

Strategy #13: *Coordinate with Colleagues* Coordinate your marketing efforts with colleagues to avoid approaching the same employers by mistake. Establish a routine procedure whereby employer contact information is regularly disseminated to colleagues.

Strategy #14: *Keep Track of Your Contacts* Develop and maintain a system for keeping track of each of your contacts. Include information about when you contacted them, the purpose of the contact, and the outcomes. The system should facilitate documentation of efforts and thus should enable you to accurately and efficiently recontact employer representatives.

One way in which to do this is to maintain a three-ring binder divided and subdivided into months and weeks, respectively. When you make a contact, keep notes pertaining to its nature and outcome (along with any other useful information). Place this sheet in the section designated for the month following the date of initial contact. When you reach this point in your notebook, you will be reminded to recontact this person. Then, update your notes and repeat the process as appropriate.

Strategy #15: *Adapt Your Style as Needed* You must believe in what you are marketing and you must exhibit sincerity in your interactions. Sincerity is something that cannot be faked; therefore, it is important to incorporate your best personal attributes into your professional approach in developing a style that works well for you. Fortunately, the strategies outlined in this chapter lend themselves to many different styles of delivery.

It is equally important to remember that every contact person has his or her own personal style as well. Some people who are very efficient and organized may seem abrupt or even unfriendly. When you encounter such a person, be business-like, come straight to the point, and avoid idle chat. Conversely, another person may be gregarious and eccentric. Follow his or her lead and allow yourself to converse about non–work-related topics, at all times being prepared to discuss business at a moment's notice.

Strategy #16: *Build "Credit" with Your Business Partners* In ascertaining an employer's needs, you will likely learn of concerns you may not have expected (e.g., a need for more information about the ADA or specific problems with a current employee). Present yourself as a resource in dealing with these concerns. The employer's contact person will thus remember you and will likely contact you should job openings come up. In essence, you are building credit with that employer.

Strategy #17: *Avoid Selling What People Don't Want* Effective job placement professionals offer a range of services to employers. In other words, they provide prospective customers with options and choices. It is a proven fact that most people respond favorably to options. One of those options may in fact be to not be interested in utilizing your agency's products or services.

The thing to remember as a job placement professional is that, by leaving an employer who is not interested at the present time with a good impression, the job placement professional has a good chance of having that employer contact him or her at a later time.

Strategy #18: *Ask for the Sale* With the exception of cold calling, this is probably the most difficult task for job placement professionals. We have been so conditioned to fear rejection that we tend to avoid making requests, even requests that are reasonable. To alleviate this problem, become comfortable saying such phrases as:

- [The jobseeker] and I would welcome the opportunity to meet with you. Is there a convenient time for you?
- After reviewing our services, do you think your company would be interested in working with us?
- How does [the jobseeker] compare with other applicants you have interviewed?
- I'd like to contact you in several weeks. When would be a good time to call?
- How well did [the jobseeker's] interview go? Your feedback would be very useful.
- Do you have any concerns about [the jobseeker]?

Expand and field test this list of phrases. Ultimately, develop phrases that suit your personal style.

CONCLUSION

A vast amount has been written in business literature regarding marketing strategies ranging from very basic and simple concepts to highly technical and statistical procedures. However, very little has been written about the use of marketing strategies for professionals in the job placement field. Nevertheless, there are three critical components of effective marketing for the job placement professional: 1) knowing the customer, 2) knowing products and services thoroughly, and 3) advertising the availability of products and services. Marketing necessarily involves each of these interdependent components, the latter two of which are discussed in this chapter.

REFERENCE

Levinson, J.C. (1989). *Guerrilla marketing excellence*. Boston: Houghton Mifflin Co.

Chapter 8 _____

QUALITY SERVICE AND CUSTOMER SATISFACTION IN JOB PLACEMENT

Ensuring customer satisfaction is central to sales and marketing success in any field, including job placement for people with disabilities. Building a solid customer base comprising satisfied repeat customers as well as established contacts is extremely important.

Seasoned marketers will caution that negative perceptions will be the consequence of inferior services and products. This has strong implications for job placement professionals. It means that, if a targeted customer (i.e., a jobseeker, employer, or other constituent) experiences or even perceives poor customer service and/or inferior quality, he or she is likely to terminate whatever working relationship exists. Worse, if the customer feels neglected, mistreated, or manipulated, he or she is very likely to tell others, thereby fueling negative public opinion for your agency.

However, if customers are pleased with your agency and its services, they will be inclined to boast to others about those services. This is in fact an efficient way to network and market.

SERVICE AND SATISFACTION

Tom Peters, the world-renowned co-author of the 1982 classic *In Search of Excellence* and author of a number of best-selling management books, believes that even customers who receive unsatisfactory outcomes may become satisfied customers if they feel that they have been treated with courtesy, respect, and a genuine attitude of helpfulness. Peters (1993) expands on this notion, saying that it is no longer simply a question of satisfying the customer. Although that may be adequate to help a business to stay relatively productive, it will not propel that business to prosperity. Businesses must "delight, thrill, and dazzle" customers (Peters, 1993). The message to the job placement professional is that, basic competence is required, but outstanding performance is what customers appreciate, remember, and ultimately publicize.

The key then is not only to convince customers that your services meet their unique needs, but to give customers the impression—based on observable, tangible results—that your services are the best services presently available. Persuading an employer to commit to using your services may seem to be the goal, but it is really just a beginning. Delivering promised goods and services in a timely and effective way is in fact the real goal.

Customer Service and Satisfaction Defined

Think of the last time that you were a customer. What were your expectations? What stands out in your mind about the customer service you received? Do you recall the service being: 1) fantastic, 2) quite acceptable, 3) fair, 4) poor, or 5) downright horrible? From a customer's perspective, we can identify things that either pleased or displeased us. We can readily pinpoint the precise action (or inaction) that took place.

Customer service should involve the full range of activities that begins with the provider's attitude and progresses through development, marketing, delivery, follow up, and evaluation. Implementation and maintenance of quality services thus occurs via one continuous feedback loop (Albin, 1992). Whether customer service is subsequently viewed by the customer as being fantastic, downright horrible, or somewhere in between, is influenced by individual professionals' understandings of customer service.

Customer satisfaction is difficult to define because it is a very subjective concept. As has been shown, there are degrees of satisfaction. Although it is a subjective phenomenon, satisfaction can be measured by formal customer surveys, informal discussions, and/or correspondence rating pleasure or displeasure with services provided. Most importantly, however, satisfaction can be measured by the degree to which customers disseminate positive information about services.

In general, people are satisfied when the products and/or services they receive benefit them—or are perceived to benefit them—in some distinct way, however large or small.

Strategies to Facilitate Customer Service and Satisfaction

Delivery of quality products and services leads ultimately to customer satisfaction. Perhaps more importantly, input from satisfied or even dissatisfied customers can guide quality improvement and innovation.

At TransCen, through that time-proven method of trial and error, a number of strategies that lead to quality services have been developed. The reader is cautioned to avoid perceiving quality as being synonymous with perfection. No human endeavor is ever completely perfect. We have all purchased products and services once that seemed perfect, but that were ultimately replaced by something better—something new and improved. As Alvin Toffler points out in his book *Power Shift* (1990), changes occur so rapidly that a quality product or service—brilliantly planned and executed 1 day—is rendered obsolete the next day. Innovators must thus anticipate change and take action. Perhaps it is this quick and proactive response to changing needs—and the rapid use of new knowledge—that is the key to achieving quality.

According to W. Edwards Deming—the American management wizard greatly credited with helping Japanese businesses to flourish—quality is whatever customers want and need (Walton, 1986). Because these wants and needs are always changing, quality solutions must continually change as well. This requires diligent and thorough research of customers' desires, issues, and concerns.

The following are several practical strategies in this regard. They are practical, common sense ideas that can be used immediately for many job placement initiatives.

Strategy #1:   Adopt a Positive Attitude that Focuses on Customer Service   People's attitudes are formulated by many factors: psychological, biological, and environmental. These attitudes necessarily influence actions. The 5-year-old who successfully rides his bike down the street by himself is guided by a certain attitude, just as is the multi-billion dollar investment banker who takes bold risks. Indeed, even organizations and enterprises may be predicated on similar confident attitudes.

For job placement professionals to succeed, certain attitudes must exist:

1.   A strong belief in the jobseeker
2.   An attitude that anything is possible
3.   A commitment to customers.

Embracing these attitudes is critical to the work of job placement. For every action, ensure that it is motivated by a sincerely positive desire to please the customer. In addition, be responsive with regard to customers' perceptions of services being received.

Strategy #2:   Solicit Complaints   Human nature being what it is, most of us do everything we can to avoid negative experiences. Complaints from others often tend to be received negatively. However, complaining customers are a valuable asset to job placement professionals. The premise is simple: a customer complains because he or she honestly believes that you can do something to mitigate a problem or a troublesome situation.

Peters (1987) points out that a "well-handled problem or complaint from a customer usually breeds more loyalty than you had before the complaint" (p. 112). Unfortunately, the complaining customer tends to be feared by professionals. However, ignoring this customer results in a disenchanted customer who just goes away mad—a person from whom you never hear another word. Nevertheless, this customer will ultimately provide you and your agency with enough bad publicity and negative marketing to undermine a great deal of effort. If the customer gives you an opportunity to fix the problem and you are able to facilitate a solution, however, you have an ally who is likely to become one of your biggest supporters. Even if you are unable to fix the problem, simply being attentive and making a sincere effort can result in the same outcome. The following list outlines several ways in which to encourage customers' feedback and complaints.

- Establish a clear, well-known policy whereby you are open to receiving feedback from any customer, regardless of the customer or the circumstances.
- Provide a number of ways by which customers may give feedback (e.g., telephone, facsimile machine, surveys, interviews, focus groups).
- Encourage customers to complain immediately when they are displeased or concerned.
- Listen! Do not argue or become defensive. Take note of specific problems being expressed.
- Nobody ever wins arguments with customers. Even if you know the customer is wrong, make him or her feel that he or she is right. Sometimes a complaining customer just wants to be heard.

Each weekly meeting with the job placement staff at TransCen begins with each attendant being asked to: 1) inform the group of any achievements made during the previous week, and 2) identify any complaints recently received from any customer (i.e., jobseekers, employers, parents, agency representatives, or colleagues). At first, few people responded—a typical human avoidance technique. As it became apparent that this procedure was permanent, however, staff began to share successes, large and small, and to encourage one another to learn from mistakes. Significantly, staff began to perceive customer complaints less as complaints and more as opportunities to continually improve services, both as individuals and as an organization.

For instance, every employer who hires a young person with a disability through the Marriott Foundation's *Bridges . . . from school to work* program is surveyed in an effort to discover what they liked about the services received from the *Bridges* staff. Moreover, every employer is asked to suggest how services may be improved. The results have been consistently enlightening: staff have been praised and terrific ideas have been generated for making services even better.

Unfortunately, traditional performance evaluations have dampened much, if not all, enthusiasm regarding the active solicitation of feedback. However, successful businesses are learning to tap into this extremely valuable source of information, which, if taken to heart, may facilitate innovations that generate new excitement and success.

Strategy #3: Respond Quickly As a customer, there is nothing more annoying than to expect goods and services at a certain time and to end up waiting, with no warning and no sense that the provider is even concerned about the delay. It may be equally as annoying to have something go wrong with a product or service and to be unable to find someone who can help you promptly. However, in the regular day-to-day delivery of goods and services, a quick response time can mean the difference between making or losing a sale, or between keeping or losing a customer. Indeed, government and giant business bureaucracies often have been undermined by competitors precisely because their cumbersome organizational structures made quick response impossible (Toffler, 1990).

Unfortunately, the human services field is notorious for slow response—not the kind of slow response that comes from careful study and concern with quality, but the kind that comes from complacency, a "business as usual" mentality, a "thinly disguised contempt" for the customer (Ford, 1993), an extensive organizational hierarchy that renders service providers powerless, or a lack of accountability. Many direct service professionals believe that agencies are responsible for this general inability to get things done in a timely manner, thus further promulgating a sense of powerlessness on the parts of individual professionals.

As we strive to improve the field of human services, however, new business standards requiring efficiency and effectiveness must be adopted. There are many activities that individuals within agencies can perform to respond in this regard. The following list outlines several examples.

- Return telephone calls promptly, within 24 hours or before the end of the business day, if possible. When you call someone right back, he or she usually expresses real surprise and appreciation, each of which is a great impression-builder.
- In cases of emergency or other pressing situations, drop everything and respond immediately. This often means negotiating with a colleague to assist.

(continued)

- If an employer or other customer calls with a problem that may require negotiation, personally attend to finding a solution. Sometimes your physical presence mitigates a tenuous situation and restores a customer's confidence in you as a resource.
- Respond quickly to correspondence, confirm appointments 1 day ahead of time, and respond promptly to requests from colleagues.
- Be energetic. Any work that involves customer contact and service is basically show business. Imagine that you pay to see a Broadway musical comedy featuring a big-name star. How would you feel if the star can't sing, isn't funny, or whines about how lousy he feels? You would probably feel cheated. The same holds true for our customers when we deal with them in a sluggish, tired, beat upon, worn out, noncreative, or patronizing manner.
- Work efficiently. Stephen Covey (1989) cautions against "time management" in his book, *The 7 Habits of Highly Effective People.* He says that the real issue is "personal management" (i.e., how we manage our activities in the time we have, how we decide what is important to us personally as well as professionally, how we determine our priorities, how we seek assistance and collaboration, and how we plan our activities weekly rather than daily).

Strategy #4: Customize Your Services With increased competition and greater product and service choice for customers, companies who are able to respond quickly and accurately to rapidly changing demands will ultimately prosper. Indeed, customers are most interested in themselves and in how products and services can be beneficial to them (Levinson, 1993; McCormack, 1984; Peters, 1987).

This situation is analogous to recent events occurring in the fields of education and human services. Increasing numbers of customers are demanding customization —new methods of service delivery that meet individually unique needs—as opposed to standardization. As the issue of choice continues to heat up (i.e., empowering people with disabilities to demand services that address their individual needs and desires), agencies espousing standardization will become obsolete, their clientele abandoning them for agencies providing more flexible service delivery. Job placement professionals must therefore shift and modify service packages in order that they may respond directly to customers' priorities, those of both jobseekers and employers. The following list outlines several tips for customizing services.

- Meet with colleagues at all levels and discuss the importance of customization. Generate examples of how services might be customized for various situations. Remain open to new ideas.
- Listen! Tailoring services implies a firm understanding of what customers want. Suppose you are altering a suit for a customer. You may think that your customer looks better in cuffed pants, but if he's telling you that he doesn't want cuffs, you must give him suit pants with no cuffs.
- Of course, you may suggest options and alternatives. In fact, an effective strategy is to demonstrate several different products or services, asking the customer to try each before making a final purchase.
- Bend the rules. This may seem controversial, but it does not imply doing something unethical or in bad taste. Rather, we are referring to using professional judgment in offering services that are within the scope of your organization's mission, but that may not have been tried previously. For example, a job placement professional was frustrated that a jobseeker was repeatedly losing good jobs because

(continued)

transportation was unreliable. The job placement professional thus contacted a church group and recruited several retirees to drive her to and from work. In another situation, a job placement professional was working with a young adult whose father wanted him to get a job. The young man stated that he wanted to go to trade school instead. Rather than automatically following the father's wishes (and offering only job placement services as mandated by the organization), the job placement professional assisted the young man in enrolling in adult education classes of his choice, and even provided tutoring assistance.

* Be creative. Indeed, you cannot customize products and services without having creativity and problem-solving skills.

Strategy #5: Look Out for "Coffee Stains" Jan Carlzon, president of Scandinavian Airline Systems, refers to each customer encounter as a "moment of truth" and suggests that the company exists from one moment of truth to the next (Albrecht, 1988). As Levinson (1993) points out, the goal of each moment of truth is to ensure that the encounter results in customer satisfaction. Peters (1987) recalls a pilot saying that, when a passenger boards a plane and pulls down a broken tray table covered with coffee stains, her immediate reaction is to question the quality of engine maintenance and of the flight crew's expertise. Peters believes that every service provider must identify existing as well as potential "coffee stains"—those factors that negatively affect customers' opinions of an entire organization. He cautions that, in order to avoid coffee stains, quality must be the primary consideration.

Unfortunately, as with many businesses, human services agencies have their share of coffee stains. Thus, the job of staff is to identify and alleviate them, or better yet, to prevent them from occurring in the first place. The following are several classic examples of coffee stains in the job placement arena:

* After receiving a frantic call from an employer concerned about a newly placed employee with a disability, staff person "A" goes to the jobsite. He is not pleased about having to cover for his colleague who actually did the placement. At the site, he yells at the worker in front of co-workers and leaves.
* Staff person "B" establishes contact with an employer, but hastily sends out brochure materials that are badly copied and misspells the contact's name in the attached letter.
* An employer calls on a regular business day. The phone rings and rings; no one answers and no answering machine picks up. It seems that everyone went out to lunch.
* A family member and jobseeker come up to your office for a scheduled appointment. They sit down and notice the remains of a half-eaten lunch on your desk.
* You and a colleague think that you are in the office alone. You make an off-the-cuff remark about a jobseeker: "This guy's off the wall." The young man in question is standing right outside the door.
* On the way back from job coaching at a construction site, wearing muddy work boots and jeans, you decide to stop in at IBM's corporate headquarters.
* You're visiting a local business office. The employer says, "Oh, I've worked with someone from your agency before. I think her name was Sue. She was terrible." You say, "You don't have to worry about that, they fired her."
* Your agency's receptionist is out sick. Without any significant training, a staff member picks up the phone and says "Yeah? What can I help ya with?" The person calling is the vice president of a large corporation.

Strategy #6: Identify "Silk Ties" In any business, mistakes will inevitably occur. Even the most carefully planned and meticulously prepared operation can be ridden with problems. Even the finest companies have experienced foul ups resulting in customer dissatisfaction. The key to mitigating such a situation is to turn a mistake into an opportunity.

Most customers tend to have a fairly high tolerance for mistakes if there is a timely and genuine response that indicates a concerted effort to rectify the situation. Attending immediately to the problem and encouraging feedback from dissatisfied customers are essential. In fact, customers frequently know precisely the solution(s) they seek. Keep in mind that, even if you are not in a position to help a customer with his or her problem, helping him or her to locate a colleague who can help is a very valuable customer service technique. Subsequently monitoring the process and outcome for the customer is also required to achieve satisfactory results.

However, as Peters (1987) suggests, fixing the immediate problem may not be sufficient. Innovative organizations have realized the added value of exceeding customers' expectations regarding repairs, solutions, or new products. Indeed, going the extra mile after a problem has been remedied has tremendous public relations value. Peters (1987) refers to these additional customer services as "silk tie" incentives.

Peters (1987) recounts a customer encounter with Nordstrom department store that demonstrates the silk tie incentive. A businessman from Portland, Oregon, was leaving on a trip and needed two new suits. His wife and daughter, devotees of this department store, encouraged him to purchase them there. The businessman went in, ordered the suits, and was assured that they would be ready by 5 P.M. the next day. Returning the following day, the customer learned that the suits were not ready as promised. Annoyed, but willing to forgive, he left on his trip. Upon arrival at his hotel in Dallas, the customer was called by the front desk to pick up a package. Two Federal Express boxes had been shipped by Nordstrom. They contained the new suits—beautifully pressed—along with two shirts and three silk ties that he had not ordered.

Clearly, Nordstrom has the resources to send such elaborate gifts to customers who experience problems. There are also thousands of small, inexpensive examples of silk ties. What's important is that two distinct things occurred: 1) a quick response to the immediate problem, and 2) something extra that let the customer know that Nordstrom cared enough about him both as a person and as a customer.

In most cases when a mistake occurs, the result is inconvenience and aggravation for the customer. Quick response followed by some form of silk tie is a proven method for fostering customer satisfaction. The following are a few examples of potential silk ties for the job placement field:

- A staff member failed to show up for an important meeting with an employer. You ensure that apologies are provided and arrange for complimentary copies of information regarding ADA to be sent to the employer.
- One of your job coaches is informed that an employee didn't show up for work recently. The next day, you pick her up, make sure she's early for work, and bring a dozen doughnuts for co-workers.
- In appreciation of a printing company hiring two jobseekers whom your agency represents, you arrange to have your brochures printed by that company.
- You notice that an employer with whom you work is mentioned in a local newspaper article. You clip the article and send it to the employer with a note.

Strategy #7: Convert Basic Competence into Outstanding Performance We have all been customers of average companies—those that provide a fairly decent product or service at a reasonable price with passable service. These companies struggle day-to-day just to attain a decent profit margin (Ford, 1989). Conversely, there are companies that sell similar products and services at reasonable prices (perhaps at prices greater than those of competitors), but that attain stellar results on a regular basis.

Certainly, job placement professionals must be competent. However, the true challenge is to exceed mere competence and to continually strive to improve efforts, at both an individual and an organizational level. Mere competence may suffice, but as funds grow tighter and consumers become more demanding, agencies and professionals who demonstrate excellence will be the winners.

Peters (1987) describes outstanding performance in terms of four levels of the Total Product Concept—a concept that can be applied to supported employment programs. The first of these levels is the *generic product*. For instance, many supported employment programs provide this first level service to employers—placing individuals with disabilities in jobs. The next level, *expected* service, is when supported employment programs operate ethically and match employees with appropriate jobs. At the third level, *augmented* service, supported employment programs provide excellent service to companies not only by placing jobseekers into jobs, but also by providing assistance to employers, as needed. At the highest level, *potential* services are offered by those few supported employment programs that operate at peak service performance. These programs often deliver resources that are essential to employers, thereby causing employers to rely on those programs (e.g., employers may rely on staff to interview jobseekers from other employment programs).

Strategy #8: Learn from Other Fields There is a tendency in every professional field to associate most often with other people in, to attend conferences particular to, and to read literature and listen to programs unique to that field.

However, tapping outside resources leads to "a cross-pollination of ideas" (Peters, 1987). It may even be a good idea to engage in "creative swiping"—imitating and improving upon the ideas of others. Indeed, every company does this to some degree.

The following box provides several suggestions of ways in which to learn from other professional fields.

- Read current literature relevant to other disciplines, particularly psychology, business, marketing, and social science.
- Keep abreast of changing social concerns and trends; consider how these trends affect your work and how your work addresses related issues.
- Attend conferences relevant for other fields; for example, job placement professionals could attend conferences or workshops sponsored by advertising associations.
- Read sections of the newspaper that you do not ordinarily read.
- Take undergraduate and graduate courses.
- Organize joint staff development training opportunities with other agencies, organizations, and businesses.
- Do volunteer work or take a leave of absence from your current job to explore another occupational field.

Strategy #9: Cultivate a Sense of Humor The best customer service is performed by people who are creative, energetic, innovative, patient, and attuned to the world around them, and humor is very much a function of each of these. It is not only a proven stress-releaser, it is a solution-generator as well.

Metcalf (1992) wrote a book titled *Lighten Up* aimed primarily at uptight business people. His message is essentially to have fun whenever possible. The pessimist may be right in the long run, but the optimist has more fun along the way.

There are certainly situations in which seriousness is required. Fortunately, however, most situations, even those encountered in a work setting, are best handled with humor. Metcalf (1992) recounts the story of an airline pilot who managed to effectively crash land a severely damaged jet loaded with passengers. Just before hitting the ground, the pilot laughed to the air traffic controller: "You say it has to be a runway?"

Strategy #10: Treat Colleagues as Customers Ironically, in many businesses, two groups are consistently overlooked: co-workers within businesses and colleagues across businesses. All business enterprises—whether profit or nonprofit, public or private, big or small—rely on: 1) teamwork within the business (Quick, 1992), and 2) suppliers and experts from other businesses. Review the following case scenario.

Think of any large hotel chain. Consider the teamwork that is required to operate just one hotel in that chain. Coordination and cooperation are essential. If a reservation clerk fails to communicate and work with a room attendant, guests' rooms would not be maintained in satisfactory condition.

Similarly, this hotel has business dealings with any number of other companies: food and beverage suppliers, parking services, dry cleaners, musicians, and so forth.

Whenever interdependence is a necessity—it generally is in most cases—it pays to treat colleagues as customers. Rosenbluth and Peters (1992) put forth the notion that highly effective organizations actually put their own employees first. That is, they have learned that utilizing a customer service mentality in dealings with co-workers at all levels pays off many times over.

Strategy #1 iterates the importance of adopting an attitude that focuses on customer service. Have you ever scheduled a meeting with a colleague only to have him or her come late or not at all, without even bothering to notify you? Conversely, have you ever refused to help a colleague with a task because you felt that you were too busy with your own work or that it was not your responsibility? These are just two of many examples where colleagues have taken each other for granted, thereby missing opportunities to foster teamwork, camaraderie, and mutual respect. The following case examples further illustrate this concept.

Tammy, a representative who worked for a job placement agency about 20 miles from her house, had to rely on public transportation to get to work each day because she has a visual impairment. Although public transportation was adequate, she frequently spent over an hour each way commuting. During a service agency coordinating meeting, she met Maggie, a representative for another agency. Realizing that they lived in the same neighborhood and worked within a mile of one another, Maggie arranged to drive Tammy to work each day.

This story clearly illustrates the concept of treating your colleagues as customers.

A similar example involves Jeremy: one day, Jeremy was backed up on appointments and called Trina, a co-worker, for assistance. Trina pitched in by taking a job-seeker on an employment interview. Jeremy made sure that he sent a thank you note to Trina, and he sent a copy of that note to her supervisor as well.

Strategy #11: **Keep Listening** Miller, Heiman, and Tuleja (1987) describe a typical sales call as "the 80% syndrome" (p. 65). They mean that, on average, a salesperson will spend over 80% of his or her time talking with a customer and less than 20% listening to that customer. This syndrome may be descriptive of job placement efforts, during which the need to outline information regarding agencies, services, and job-seekers takes precedence over listening to customers' expectations and needs. However, in order to assess how and if an agency's services match customers' expectations, it is necessary to do less talking and more listening. Moreover, in order to evaluate how well agencies' services meet customers' expectations, it is imperative to keep listening.

CONCLUSION

This chapter presents strategies necessary for providing quality service and achieving customer satisfaction. Several of these strategies such as looking out for coffee stains and identifying silk ties could be enacted immediately. Others may take longer to put into practice. Regardless, it is important that job placement agencies move toward accomplishing at least one of these strategies as soon as possible. This will invariably improve customers' perceptions of those agencies.

The importance of customers' perceptions cannot be overemphasized. Peters (1987) advises to view "every element of every operation through the customer's lens" and to "constantly attempt to redefine each element of the business in terms of the customer's perception of the intangibles" (p. 123). This is equally important for job placement professionals.

One way in which to view services "through the customer's lens" is to solicit feedback from customers regarding the services they received. Ask them, "How are we doing?" and then be prepared to listen. Listening to customers as they describe perceptions and reactions is an excellent strategy for promoting customer responsiveness. Conversely, becoming defensive, resistant, or angry will have the opposite effect. Remember that little things mean a great deal to customers. Listening honestly to their kudos and complaints about an agency and its services will go a long way toward facilitating customer satisfaction in the future.

REFERENCES

Albin, J. (1992). *Quality improvement in employment and other human services.* Baltimore: Paul H. Brookes Publishing Co.

Albrecht, C. (1988). *At America's service.* New York: Warner Books.

Covey, S.R. (1989). *The 7 habits of highly effective people.* New York: Simon & Schuster.

Ford, L. (Speaker). (1989). *How to give exceptional customer service* [Videocassette]. Boulder, CO: CareerTrack Publications.

Levinson, J.C. (1993). *Guerrilla marketing excellence.* Boston: Houghton Mifflin Co.

McCormack, M.H. (1984). *What they don't teach you at Harvard Business School.* New York: Bantam Books.

Metcalf, C.W. (1992). *Lighten up.* Reading, MA: Addison-Wesley.

Peters, T. (1987). *Thriving on chaos.* New York: Harper Perennial.

Peters, T. (Speaker). (1993). *The new manager and the new organization* (Cassette recording). Boulder, CO: CareerTrack Publications.

Peters, T., & Waterman, R. (1982) *In search of excellence.* New York: Bantam Books.

Quick, T.L. (1992). *Successful team building.* New York: American Management Association.

Rosenbluth, H.F., & Peters, D.M. (1992). *The customer comes second.* New York: William Morrow and Co.

Toffler, A. (1990). *Power shift.* New York: Bantam Books.

Walton, M. (1986). *The Deming management method.* New York: Perigee Books.

SECTION III

INTO THE FUTURE

Chapter 9

BUSINESS CONSULTATION— AN EMERGING ROLE FOR JOB PLACEMENT PROFESSIONALS

Changing demographics and the resultant emphasis on workforce investment will ultimately create altogether new circumstances for American business in the future as it attempts to make the best use of a diverse workforce (National Alliance of Business, 1992; Tucker, 1992). These circumstances have already been the impetus behind the formation of a number of entrepreneurial enterprises designed to help businesses to react to and prepare for profound changes in workforce management. Principal among these enterprises are those that provide personnel management consultation. In fact, Kleiman (1992) suggests that management consultation, including activities that involve "training a diverse workforce and helping firms meet employee's work and family needs" (p. 129), will become one of the fastest growing occupational categories in the 1990s. This growth could represent significant opportunity for job placement professionals. Unfortunately, the wisdom of the job placement field remains largely hidden from business. In fact, job placement professionals are traditionally apologetic when approaching employers. This suggests that they believe that business is unlikely to be interested in their talents or those of the people they represent.

The "hire the handicapped" campaigns of the early 1970s have been replaced by appeals that are only slightly less reliant on charitable appeals. Slogans like "What people with disabilities need is a chance" and "These people are so grateful to be working that they are more reliable than the average employee" are not unusual in job placement marketing materials. This, coupled with the fact that job placement staff are typically inexperienced and uncomfortable in dealing with the business world, means that employers have not turned to job placement professionals to solve their human resource problems.

However, considering the challenges that business faces in the future, the job placement profession may be an invaluable source of human resource consultants who have legitimate skills that can meet business's needs. Similarly, business's efforts to recruit, select, train, and motivate employees would benefit from such additional expertise in job analysis and matching, task analysis, training technology, and positive behavior shaping. Conversely, knowledge regarding the preparation of people with disabilities for the workplace can be redirected to better prepare the workplace for people with disabilities. This will in turn prevent workplace assimilation for people with disabilities from being one-sided.

JOB PLACEMENT PROFESSIONALS AS CONSULTANTS

Businesses solicit the aid of consultants in cases where they require: special knowledge and skills, intensive help on a temporary basis, an impartial outside viewpoint, justification for management decisions, remedial instruction, information about how to improve their benefits-to-cost ratio, and/or help in solving a problem (Kubr, 1986). Essentially, they seek expertise they do not have.

It is apparent that consultants offer a variety of resources and information to businesses. However, Shenson (1990) points out that many consulting companies fail because they market only the technical aspects of their services. The same might be said of traditional attempts of job placement agencies to market services to businesses; they often have mistakenly gone to great lengths to describe for employers the technical aspects of their services (e.g., vocational evaluation, work adjustment training, and job coaching). However, according to experienced consultants, it is critical to approach potential business partners regarding particular needs (e.g., vacant positions, a lack of knowledge regarding diversity issues, decreased productivity, a cumbersome work flow, or poor sales).

A highly competent technical expert in computer network applications was so confident in his abilities that he quit his job to become an independent consultant. After 5 months, however, he gained only one client and soon after was forced to abandon his enterprise. The reason? It was certainly not due to either a lack of expertise or a depressed market for computer network applications. In fact, such experts are in considerable demand. His mistake, it seemed, was that he approached his prospective clients reciting, in very esoteric terms, all of the technical aspects of his services—memory capacity of the network he installed, features of the hardware he preferred, and potential software applications. However, prospective clients were interested in sharing data, storing information, and generating reports. Although he impressed them, he wasn't able to show them how his technical knowledge could be used to solve their problems.

The success of both job placement professionals and business consultants is predicated upon a strong orientation to customers' needs. Shenson (1990) likens this to the experience of choosing a five-star restaurant: "As a patron, you expect to be served a fine meal with decorum and taste. The frantic conditions of the kitchen are not your concern, nor should they be" (p. 5).

A job placement professional made several calls on a large discount department store ostensibly to find out what jobs it had and how it did them so he could prepare people served by his agency for such occupations. Over the course of several visits, the job placement professional noticed that, whenever a delivery of clothing merchandise was made to the store, several sales associates from the clothing department were required to assist in the unloading and stacking of that incoming merchandise. They would subsequently remove the clothing from the boxes, strip off the cellophane covering individual articles, and rehang the articles on new hangers for display in the store. During this process, customers in the clothing department had no one to assist them; therefore, sales were lost.

However, the job placement professional had been working with a young lady who would be suited to work in the receiving area accepting the incoming clothing merchandise, thereby allowing the sales associates to remain in the clothing department to assist customers. The job placement professional suggested that the cost of hiring the young lady would be more than offset by the increase in sales that would result from more attention on the sales floor.

The result? The young lady had the first paying job of her life and the store had in fact increased its sales—a problem identified and solved by a consultant. He never once focused on his technical expertise; rather, he simply responded to his customers' needs.

What Good Consultants Do

The following is a list of commonly identified business consultant activities (Barcus & Wilkinson, 1986; Cohen, 1985; Greenbaum, 1990; Shenson, 1990; Shenson & Nichols, 1993):

- *Instruct* clients in new techniques. Businesses spend billions of dollars per year on consultants who can teach employees what they need to know. In fact, human resource management training represents one of the most widely used types of business consultation.
- *Demonstrate* new techniques. Sometimes instruction must be coupled with demonstration—how to use a new computer software program or how to structure a product assembly sequence.
- *Facilitate* decision making and planning. Solving specific problems often requires intensive planning. Similarly, the launching of a new product line ultimately requires objective decision making that can best be facilitated by an outside consultant. Focus groups conducted by consultants are good examples of this.
- *Communicate* new ideas or clarify old ones. Communication is universally recognized as the single most important skill any consultant can have (Cohen, 1985; Golen, 1986; Shenson, 1990). Consultants may be asked to arbitrate disputes, negotiate agreements, handle difficult people, and even translate business's jargon. Also, written documents, such as reports, letters of agreement, and trade newsletters, represent important consultant tools for communicating with business clients.
- *Assess* organizational needs. Assessing relevant circumstances is a necessary preliminary to problem resolution (i.e., What is the problem and what can be done about it?). Additionally, consultants are often asked to look at the needs of a company as a prelude to, or in conjunction with, training.
- *Prepare* business clients to do for themselves. The most effective consultants are those who provide consultation and subsequently step aside.

- *Conduct an inventory* of internal expertise, skills, and interests. If the consultant is to leave business clients able to do for themselves, then finding out who in the company is best suited to assume new or expanded responsibility is often necessary.
- *Follow up* after consultation is provided. The best consultants, like the best businesses, are those who provide service after the sale. This not only contributes to long-term relationships—an essential ingredient of any successful business partnership—but also results in repeat business and strong referrals for new business (Miller & Heiman, 1985).

The action verbs that begin each point above could easily be ascribed to any number of traditional job placement activities. Job placement professionals are instructors, evaluators, facilitators, mentors, communicators and listeners, demonstrators, and educators, just to name a few. These professionals just need to learn how to apply these skills in new ways.

Let's take a look at how these consultant activities can be applied in efforts to promote employment for people with disabilities.

Instruction   Instruction is a critical element of almost all job placement programs, and job placement professionals, for the most part, are very good at it. Unfortunately, this highly developed skill is most often applied only to jobseekers with disabilities. However, it can become a valuable tool for employers and businesses as well.

Regarding TransCen's work with Southland Corporation, an employee assistance program specialist was trained in the personnel department to take advantage of the resources of job placement agencies in recruiting applicants with learning disabilities. This person was also taught how to instruct store managers and supervisors in training, accommodating, and supervising these workers. As a result, over 40 new placements were made in the 2-year course of consultation.

Similarly, since 1991, TransCen's staff have conducted over 200 training sessions with employers regarding interviewing techniques. These sessions are designed to help personnel managers understand: 1) what ADA requires when considering applicants with disabilities, 2) the preferred etiquette for interacting with people with disabilities, and 3) how to ask questions that help determine if applicants can perform essential job functions. It is important to note that employers have paid for these services.

Instruction as a consultation tool assumes many forms (e.g., disability awareness training). For example, Milt Wright and Associates, a California-based consulting firm, has trained literally thousands of employers in disability awareness and related topics.

Demonstration   When working with employers, it is often necessary to demonstrate specific job accommodations. For example, one young man was hired as an assistant store clerk. Among other responsibilities, he was required to inventory and stock shelves. However, every time he was given more than two instructions at a time, he would act as if he understood but would invariably make critical mistakes. He needed one-step oral directions accompanied by written instructions. Once the store manager saw this supervisory approach applied by an experienced job placement professional, he had no further problem with the employee.

In another case, a supervisor called the employment specialist who placed an individual in his company. This individual was performing so poorly that he would be fired if he did not improve. However, when the supervisor was shown how to rearrange the presentation of the material—simply reversing the direction of a circuit board on an assembly table so that it was easier to grasp by the employee—he noted an immediate improvement in the employee's performance. The employee was retained.

Scenarios like these occur each day. Many jobs have been saved and many employers have improved their supervisory approach as a result of such effective demonstrations by job placement professionals.

Facilitation A rapidly growing electroplating company went in just 2 years from employing 5 to employing over 250 individuals. This growth created several problems for the newly established personnel department, which handled not only employee selection for the company, but also ensured compliance with personnel laws and regulations. The company was especially concerned about the ADA. The vice president of personnel said, "We have so many needs and so many questions, we don't know where to start" (C. Barnes, personal communication, February, 1993).

After several meetings, it was agreed that the best way to proceed was to survey the managers concerning the problems and issues they were encountering. A series of planning sessions was facilitated, and several major concerns were identified: fear that the ADA was simply a burdensome federal law designed to complicate their jobs, discomfort regarding disability issues, fear that an onslaught of unqualified applicants was forthcoming, and anxiety about adding more responsibilities to already hectic jobs. These planning sessions led to decisions to: 1) develop a brief, easy-to-follow guide to the ADA so that managers would not be required to spend a lot of time in digesting its intricacies; 2) train managers in interviewing techniques; and 3) designate one supervisor to attend several seminars on the ADA so as to become an informed internal resource when managers and supervisors had questions about personnel actions as they related to the ADA. It was subsequently decided, however, to have all supervisors participate in disability awareness training. Thus, from this group—originally skeptical about disability issues and the ADA—emerged individuals who eventually were instrumental in the company's hiring several people represented by local job placement agencies.

Communication Using communication skills in consultation with employers is very important. Consider the following two scenarios.

A supported employment job coach was supervising the performance of an individual who was working at a local fast food restaurant. This individual was responsible for stocking the salad bar and cleaning the dining area. The manager of the restaurant observed that this worker would frequently behave in socially inappropriate ways when the job coach was not present. He subsequently told the job coach: "He performs and behaves well when you're here. As soon as you leave he will lay on the floor in front of the salad bar or follow customers around. What should I do?" The job coach agreed to spend time in training the individual to stay on task and to perhaps even develop a behavior program that would consequate inappropriate behavior. The coach made several follow-up visits, designed a mutually acceptable "behavior contract" that specified rewards for on-task behavior, and provided counseling concerning the desirability of appropriate behavior in the workplace. Unfortunately, however, the problem behaviors persisted and the manager eventually terminated the employee.

* * *

An employment specialist developed a job for a young adult at a microfiche company. From the very beginning, the employment specialist began teaching the company's staff how to structure assignments, how to provide feedback, and what to say

---

(continued)

when the young adult goes off task. The interaction occurred primarily between the specialist and the employer in the context not only of communicating to the employer (i.e., educating and demonstrating) how to interact with the young adult, but also listening to how the employer wanted to get the job done. Essentially, the specialist's communication skills were used to help the employer learn how to train, supervise, and accommodate the employee. That is, the employer received consultation from the employment specialist.

Although the two scenarios reflect an oversimplification of the circumstances, who's to say that the failure of the first employee wasn't due to a bad job match or other factors? The fact is that the second employer received the benefit of a competent consultant skilled in the management of a person who turned out to be a valued employee. In the first example, communication occurred only with the employee: the employer felt powerless to act unless the job coach was there. More importantly, the job coach did not seem to hear the employer when he asked, "What should *I* do?" Listening to the question may have caused the job coach to take a whole different approach, which may have involved the manager and the other employees in identifying and delivering consequences for behaviors.

Assessment Assessment of the skills, interests, and aptitudes of jobseekers with disabilities is one of the most widely applied job placement practices. Vocational evaluation, assistive technology assessments, and work adjustment training have traditionally received a great deal of emphasis as well. These prevalent approaches, and their accompanying bodies of knowledge and skills, can also be utilized as consultant tools.

United Cerebral Palsy (UCP) of New Jersey has developed an exciting process to assess the assistive technology needs at the workplace of people with significant physical disabilities. The process—Televideo Assessment—was devised to provide an "in vivo" approach to prescribing applications for appropriate assistive devices. Although this approach represents a great advantage to jobseekers, it also has considerable potential as a consultation tool that directly benefits employers.

Bertha is a 20-year-old graduate of special education who uses a motorized wheelchair. As part of her educational experience prior to graduation, Bertha was spending part of her school day as a part-time mail courier for a local company. It was determined that job modifications and assistive technology would be necessary in order for her to perform the requirements of the job. Her teacher videotaped her daily routine and sent a copy [of the tape] to be reviewed by a rehabilitation technology team associated with UCP of New Jersey.

A telephone conference was scheduled at the worksite. Bertha, her employer, and her teacher subsequently were connected to the rehabilitation technology team via telephone, and both groups simultaneously viewed and discussed Bertha's work and possible modifications. During the conference, the rehabilitation technology team made specific recommendations for modifications and technology. Each suggestion was discussed in detail with all parties involved; a plan was developed to make modifications to Bertha's wheelchair and to restructure her office environment (i.e., applying Velcro to the mail carrying case for stabilization, lowering shelves, moving mail slots to a lower position, and rearranging Bertha's workspace for greater accessibility). As a result of this assessment and the subsequent modifications and applications of technology, Bertha's performance increased and she was offered a permanent position with the company.

One veteran job placement professional said when told of Bertha's circumstance: "Isn't it great that she received the benefit of this new approach?" (M. Larson, personal communication, June, 1993). One might ask, isn't it also great that her employer was a direct recipient of such valuable consultation? After all, this assessment was provided at the place of employment with the input of the employer; Bertha did not have to travel to a specially equipped center, nor was the employer forced to wait until a specially trained team of technologists could travel to the worksite. Thus, technology brought the consultation directly to the employer—a problem solved for the employer as well.

Preparation "The only work worth doing as a consultant is that which educates—which teaches clients and their staff to manage better for themselves" (Lyndon Urwick, as cited in Kubr, 1986).

During the first 2 years of TransCen's association with Southland, a critical role of the Southland employee assistance program (EAP) specialist was to provide awareness training as well as on-site instruction to supervisors and store managers concerning both the nature of learning disabilities and specific accommodations that could be provided for employees with learning disabilities. It was TransCen's responsibility to provide training and consultation to the EAP specialist, who was thus prepared to maintain the program after the consultation ended.

Her role as the company's designated disability trainer and expert continued well beyond the consultation. In fact, she extended her reach within the company far beyond the parameters of the project as originally conceived. Thus, Southland no longer depends on an outside expert in disability issues after TransCen's consultation. As one Southland executive put it, "Equipping our company to adequately manage the diversity that exists in our present and future workforce is a major priority. Understanding disability and developing confidence and competence in supervising employees with disabilities are important tools of human resource management" (D. Wilner, personal communication, June, 1990).

When TransCen's formal consulting relationship with Southland ended, Southland was left to manage on its own. Enabling the corporation to hire, train, and accommodate applicants with disabilities has paid dividends in terms of job placements for people with disabilities long after TransCen was removed from the picture.

A further example of this concept is the Skills Training Partnership (STP) initiated by the Canadian Council on Rehabilitation and Work. Through the STP, employers identify occupational categories that they consistently need to fill, and training programs are subsequently designed. STP representatives, employers, and training institutions jointly plan these training programs for jobseekers with disabilities in order that they can be prepared for the identified occupations. In Toronto, for example, the Bank of Montreal hired 15 individuals who received training specific to the Bank's teller and customer service positions. Job placement agencies from the Toronto area referred trainees, but the Bank itself designed and supervised the training after being prepared by STP consultants.

Conducting Inventory In 1988, TransCen assisted Marriott Corporation in piloting an internally operated supported employment project. The pilot called for establishing a mechanism for Marriott to hire, train, and provide ongoing support to employees with disabilities who required considerable training and supervisory support. This approach required the identification of an existing Marriott employee to perform the functions of a job trainer. The idea was that an employee who knew the needs and expectations of the company would be better equipped than an outside job placement professional to ensure job success for applicants with disabilities.

To identify such a person essentially required that a consultant assist Marriott in conducting an inventory of staff who had served in various capacities within the company and had the aptitude to be an effective job trainer for people with disabilities. After interviewing several Marriott personnel, reviewing work histories, and spending time observing various corporate operations, a person was identified. She had worked in hotels, food service, and personnel recruiting, and most importantly had no preconceived notions about people with disabilities. The inventory thus yielded a person who not only made the pilot successful, but who has subsequently received several promotions.

In a more formal sense, accessibility surveys conducted through the use of computer software such as ADAAG Express (1993) are a means by which companies can be assisted in taking an inventory of physical environments so as to both comply with Title III of the ADA and to enhance their ability to provide a more "user friendly" environment for present and future employees with disabilities. As job placement agencies and professionals offer such services to employers, they are providing consultation that facilitates expanded capabilities in accommodating employees with disabilities.

Follow Up   Since the conclusion of TransCen's consultant relationship with Southland Corporation, many occasions have arisen when advice was sought concerning specific ideas regarding accommodating jobseekers with disabilities. For example, TransCen was called when a jobseeker was being considered for a store clerk position. He was able to effectively use only his left hand, thereby making certain cash register operations problematic. However, a simple key change on the cash register provided the solution. The jobseeker was not in any way involved with TransCen, nor was TransCen obligated to provide assistance to Southland, but follow-up consultation was offered nevertheless.

Similarly, consider the following scenario: an employer had received disability awareness training from a local job placement professional. A few days after the training ended, a person who was deaf presented himself to the employer's personnel officer to apply for a job. "I panicked," she said. "Even though I had just gone through the training and felt more comfortable with the idea of interviewing a person with a disability, I had no idea how I should communicate with a deaf person." She called the job placement professional while the applicant was in the waiting room:

> I was given what now seems like the most common sense advice in the world—ask the applicant what was the best way to communicate with him. It turned out that we could communicate very well through written messages. It was a very pleasant interview and it turned out that he was over-qualified and therefore not interested in the job. What a relief it was, though, to have the job placement professional so readily available to give me advice. I learned more that day than I could have learned in several days of training. (M. Thompson, personal communication, September, 1992)

This was definitely good consultant follow up—service after the sale.

The best job placement professionals understand the importance of responsive follow up. They often call on employers after training to determine when retraining is necessary or when an additional accommodation must be identified. Indeed, the value of this follow up is as important to the employer as it is to the employee with a disability.

Seven Attributes of Outstanding Consultants

Lippert and Lippert (1986) categorize consultant qualities into two broad areas: intellectual abilities and personal and interpersonal attributes. Essentially, a good consultant has to know his or her stuff and must be able to get along with people—qualities that would be expected of any good job placement professional. However, being a good consultant and being an outstanding one are two different things. The following are seven attributes of outstanding consultants as identified by Cohen (1985). To these attributes might also be added the abilities to think on one's feet, to change if an approach is not working, to adapt to changing situations, and to be flexible in the face of changing employer demands. There are many subtleties in the applications of good consulting skills, and alertly applying appropriate skills will lead to many positive placement outcomes.

Bedside Manner   This refers to the ability to secure the confidence and trust of business clients. This often simply requires getting along with people, avoiding a know-it-all or hostile attitude, and having a demeanor that indicates helpfulness—much like a doctor who, by her approach to a patient, communicates calmness and assurance. How you say something can be as important as what you say.

The Ability to Diagnose a Problem   Before recommending a solution, accurately identifying the problem is critical. The employment specialist who showed the department store manager that sales staff were losing sales when they left the sales floor to unload deliveries diagnosed a significant problem. This is outstanding consultation.

The Ability to Find Solutions   The same employment specialist proposed a solution that worked—hire someone to receive and prepare clothing deliveries. Subsequent to diagnosis, consultation is all about finding solutions.

Technical Expertise and Knowledge   Of course, one must know one's stuff. All of the expertise represented in the field of job placement has value in a variety of ways. Applying this expertise in new ways will enhance the success of job placement.

Communication Skills   Most counseling and training programs will emphasize the importance of developing good communication and counseling skills. All experienced consultants will say that possessing good communication skills is the most important factor in a successful consultant relationship; more important, many say, than technical expertise. Recall the case example where the job coach developed several intervention strategies, but failed to consider the real concern of the restaurant manager.

Marketing and Selling Ability   As has been stated in a number of ways, providing good services is only beneficial if those services are marketed and subsequently sold. The nine keys to successful consulting in the next section focus on this issue.

Management Skills   Whether it's managing a caseload or an entire organization, the effectiveness of a consultant is enhanced by good planning, organization, and follow through.

Nine Keys to Successful Consulting

Many popular business consultant manuals identify ways in which successful consultants build and maintain fruitful partnerships with business clients (Cohen, 1985; Shenson, 1990). Below are nine ways that are most applicable to enhancing job placement professionals' effectiveness as consultants to business.

Dedication to a Marketing Orientation   Provide what the market wants, not what you think it wants. Being aware of market trends is absolutely essential. You can have it your way at Burger King because the market for fast food said that it wanted variety. Similarly, job placement should not provide ADA training if area employers already have available legal seminars on the topic. Many a business consultant regrets developing an elaborate solution to nonexistent problems (Shenson, 1990). Continually research, survey, and test the market regarding the issues and problems currently facing local employers.

Devotion to Client Interest, Above and Beyond All Other This is really customer service revisited. Be attentive to business clients' needs. Avoid the know-it-all approach and do not rely on standard sales pitches in marketing services. In other words, do not reiterate statistics about people with disabilities having high attendance rates. Rather, ask employers what their most critical needs are. Ask yourself, "How will what I do benefit the employer with whom I am working?"

Generating Rapport Before Selling Get to know the employer and establish trust. Rapport will develop as you show a genuine interest in the employer's business and its operation. For instance, when job placement professionals join local Chambers of Commerce and thereby contribute to their well-being by participating actively in their activities, the professionals are establishing rapport. They are seen as lending a hand rather than as holding their hand out; this shows a genuine interest in a community's economic cohesion. McCormack (1984) says that it is good to find some common ground with a present or prospective business client, be it a shared affinity for music, sports, and so forth, or a common interest in the community.

Dedication to Developing a Marketing Strategy Based on Creating Image and Reputation Image is projected through the "look" of a job placement agency. This includes its name (i.e., "New Hope Center" does not create a particularly positive business image), quality of printed materials, location, appearance of staff (i.e., TransCen has a dress code of business attire at all times except when on-site work requires otherwise), and professional staff conduct (Dileo & Langton, 1993). Marketing is also served well when an agency becomes involved in highly visible community activities that are outside of that agency's usual mission. For example, TransCen's staff and associates participate annually in the fund drive for a local public television station by providing people to answer phones and accept pledges on behalf of that station during an entire evening's broadcast. Staff are visible taking pledges on the bank of phones behind the announcers and TransCen's name is flashed across the screen regularly throughout the evening. Thus, an image of community service is created, publicity is generated, and a good cause is served.

Marketing Results, not Technology Another way to say this is to market results, not disability. One would never expect to see this ad placed by an employer:

Help wanted: Company looking for individual with psychiatric disability with extensive history of hospitalization. Delusional behavior okay. Supportive co-workers. Call for application.

Yet, many job placement agencies market jobseekers with disabilities in a similar way, using phrases such as "Help people with disabilities achieve independence," or "Everyone deserves a chance." It is almost as if job placement agencies are unconsciously hawking "damaged goods." What should rather be emphasized is the competency of a job placement agency and the individuals it represents, and, as a result, how prospective business clients will benefit.

Avoiding the Impression that One Is Needy The traditional, apologetic approaches of job placement professionals certainly leave employers with the impression that job placement agencies are not good business partners. However, any high-quality job placement agency or consulting service projects an impression that reflects success and past achievement. Emphasize past successes and brag about prominent employers with whom you're affiliated. Even though job placement agencies are quite anxious to gain employers' business (i.e., to get them to hire jobseekers they represent), they especially want to leave an impression that reflects confidence and success, regardless of employers' hiring decisions. Indeed, people like to associate with winners.

Being Accessible and Helpful This is really good customer service. Promptly returning phone calls, responsive follow up, and expressing a genuine interest in the nature of business's problems are some of the ways in which job placement professionals become accessible and helpful. Avoid any hint of the existence of an inefficient bureaucracy.

Devotion to the Value of Referral Marketing Good customer service solicits repeat customers, and repeat customers tell others about the quality service they receive. Ask good contacts for other contacts; better yet, ask them to make initial contacts for you. Many job placement agencies use business advisory councils not only to provide feedback and advice concerning job placement initiatives, but also to generate referrals from their business colleagues (Venne, 1992).

Consistency in Marketing No matter how good you become at attracting the interests of businesses and employers, you can never rest on past achievements. Even after placing over 200 jobseekers a year and providing consulting services (i.e., training and technical assistance) to businesses, TransCen facilitates placements and consultant contracts only through continuous marketing—seminars, newsletters, event sponsorship, surveys, and/or mailings. Marketing is an activity that requires continuous attention. In fact, any business succeeds only through continuously marketing its services or products. Would Nike sell as many athletic shoes without its logo appearing ubiquitously at televised sporting events or without the sponsorship of high profile athletes? Would Pepsi sell as many soft drinks without Ray Charles and the "Uh-Huh" girls? Would any product sell without sales representatives soliciting orders?

AN EVOLVING CONSULTANT ROLE

An increasingly popular job placement approach is the use of so-called *natural supports* (Nisbet & Hagner, 1988). The premise is that, if employees with significant disabilities are supported by means naturally existing in the workplace rather than by a job coach, they will experience increased social integration, less stigma associated with being monitored on the job, and presumably greater job success. As with any popularized approach, the idea of natural supports has been subject to considerable misinterpretation. However, if properly done, the use of natural supports is best facilitated when job placement professionals act as technical advisors and consultants. In fact, all of the consultant roles discussed in this chapter are necessary if employers are to be prepared to successfully manage and supervise employees with disabilities.

If natural supports are to have merit as an approach to service delivery, then job placement professionals must be trained in carrying out often complex and sophisticated consultant roles. In fact, any professional job placement role that entails the significant management of relationships with employers will require training that includes a strong emphasis on consulting. Otherwise, it's back to the "beg, place, and pray" model that plagues the job placement field.

CONCLUSION

This chapter outlines consulting strategies that will improve the management of relationships with employers. According to Kubr (1986), "Directly or indirectly, all changes generated and implemented with the consultant's help should contribute to improvements in the quality of management and in the organization's performance or excellence" (p. 29). When job placement professionals do this with the companies with which they interact, they are on the right track.

There seems to be endless possibility for partnerships engendered through professional consultation provided by job placement professionals. If the opportunity is seized, business will regularly solicit the consulting services of job placement professionals and agencies whose services are characterized by quality and customer responsiveness. In the end, business will come to realize job placement agencies as necessary business partners.

Business as usual for job placement will mean that significant opportunities will be missed. In fact, given decreasing government resources, it may mean no business at all. Job placement has at its disposal a wealth of knowledge and expertise that businesses not only want, as focus groups illustrate, but also need, as workforce diversity and the ADA dictate. The key will be for the job placement field to show business that by using the consultation services that job placement professionals can provide, there will be a return on investment that merits future partnerships.

REFERENCES

Barcus, S., & Wilkinson, J. (Eds.). (1986). *Handbook of managing consulting services.* New York: McGraw-Hill.

Cohen, W. (1985). *How to make it big as a consultant.* New York: AMACOM.

Dileo, D., & Langton, D. (1993). *Get the marketing edge: A job developer's toolkit.* St. Augustine, FL: Training Resource Network.

Golen, S. (1986). Effective communication skills. In S. Barcus & J. Wilkinson. (Eds.), *Handbook of management consulting services* (pp. 77–98). New York: McGraw-Hill.

Greenbaum, T. (1990). *The consultant's manual: The complete guide to building a successful consulting practice.* New York: John Wiley & Sons.

Kleiman, C. (1992). *The 100 best jobs for the 1990's and beyond.* Chicago: Dearborn Financial Publishing.

Kokomo Software, Inc. (1993). *ADAAG Express* [Computer Program]. Salt Lake City, UT: Author.

Krahn, P. (1993). Report on the Skills Training Partnership. *Ability and Enterprise, 5*(4), 18–21.

Kubr, M. (1986). *Management consulting: A guide to the profession.* Washington, DC: International Labour Office.

Lippert, C., & Lippert, R. (1986). *The consulting process in action.* San Diego, CA: University Associates.

McCormack, M. (1984). *What they don't teach you at Harvard Business School.* New York: Bantam Books.

Miller, R., & Heiman, S. (1985). *Strategic selling.* New York: Warner Books.

National Alliance of Business. (1992). *Building a workforce investment system for America.* Washington, DC: Author.

Nisbet, J., & Hagner, D. (1988). Natural supports in the workplace: A reexamination of supported employment. *Journal of The Association for Persons with Severe Handicaps, 13,* 260–267.

Shenson, H. (1990). *Shenson on consulting.* New York: John Wiley & Sons.

Shenson, H., & Nichols, T. (1993). *The complete guide to consulting success.* Chicago: Enterprise Dearborn.

Tucker, M. (1992). *A human resource plan for the United States.* Washington, DC: National Center on Education and Economics.

Venne, R. (1992). *Business advisory council: A manual for operating the best marketing system for developing supported employment opportunities for people with disabilities.* Florence, MA: Supported Employment Concepts.

Chapter 10

A NEW PARADIGM

This book is about partnerships: what they are, how to develop them, and how to redesign existing programs and practices so that they will be more responsive to business. Because of current social and political trends, we have a critical opportunity to rethink the ways in which services are delivered to people with disabilities. However, there are also critical environmental factors that can have a powerful influence on existing opportunities.

Imagine walking into a job placement or any human services agency where staff and consumers greet you politely and ask if they can be of any help. The decor is modern and like that of any business or government agency. This agency is located in a building that houses various types of private and public businesses and services. You inquire regarding available services; there is even a brochure that describes services in terms of their benefits to you as a potential customer. Nothing in the brochure hints at or implies that services are in any way related to charity, altruism, or good will.

You look around and several things stand out. For instance, many people are using a variety of technological adaptations in order to do their jobs. Telecommunication devices for the deaf (TDDs) and telephone teletypes (TTYs) are standard, and open spaces facilitate wheelchairs and other types of enabling equipment. The waiting room is busy and seems fairly standard, with one major difference: the focus is on diversity. Publications range from *U.S. News and World Report* to the *Disability Rag*. Several people are filling out job applications while others are arranging appointments using telephones, faxes, and TDDs.

One way in which to think of this current situation is in terms of Lewin's (1951) famous "force field analysis." The idea of a force field analysis is to be aware in identifying those forces that either push you toward your goals and/or hinder your attaining those goals. If the goal is to develop business partnerships in the community, it may be facilitated by political forces such as the ADA, the push for the provision of reasonable accommodations, and the increasing positive image of people with disabilities in public mass media. However, there are also negative forces that hinder attainment of this goal. A sample of these includes: a focus on service delivery as opposed to job outcomes, negative attitudes regarding the abilities of people with disabilities, and categorization of people with disabilities according to impairment.

THE FUTURE OF PARTNERSHIPS

Taking advantage of opportunities requires job placement agencies and professionals to be aware of those opportunities. Several social and economic trends that exist today have been reviewed. It is important for agencies and professionals to be aware of these trends and the ways in which they influence people with disabilities in their efforts to manage and create employment opportunities in the future.

Imagine that you are the personnel director of a corporation that will soon relocate its headquarters in the local community. You have an appointment with a personnel manager at the Jobs Plus Agency (JPA) in order to discuss what types of job placement services JPA can provide.

The personnel manager seems to know quite a bit about your business and you are pleasantly surprised because it's not often that such employment and training agencies take the time to find out about potential customers. In fact, she has already sketched out what she believes to be your personnel and business needs and is ready to discuss how JPA can fulfill those needs. She would also like to arrange a visit to your headquarters in order to take a closer look at operations and the environment.

You mention that some of your supervisory staff may not fully understand various aspects of ADA and reasonable accommodations, and the personnel manager asks one of the other staff members to come in to discuss opportunities regarding an introductory seminar on reasonable accommodations. She explains that this is part of the free-of-charge benefits for contracting with her agency. If additional technical assistance is needed, agency personnel will consult with her regarding needs and appropriate service charges.

As you leave, you are quite satisfied that you have found an experienced, knowledgeable, and responsible partner in the community. You subsequently load your wheelchair into your van and drive back to the office.

Business Trends that Influence
Employment for People with Disabilities

Shifting to customer-driven marketing approaches, changing job development and placement processes to meet customers' needs, and paying careful attention to public perceptions of services are all necessary in order for job placement agencies to develop effective partnerships. However, it is also critical to understand the trends affecting and changing the ways in which American business does business. Although some of these trends have already been examined in detail (i.e., customer satisfaction, marketing strategies, and accommodating diverse needs), there are other business trends that have implications for job placement agencies as well. These include downsizing, employee empowerment, building a sense of community at the workplace, "smaller is better," focusing on accountability and performance, mobile workforces, and investment in the future through training and lifelong learning. Each is discussed in turn.

Downsizing Career-long employment with a single corporation is no longer standard in late–20th-century America. The vision of the "corporate man" who dons his gray suit and loyally spends his entire career being promoted within one company is obsolete. The corporate man is being replaced with the corporate woman; lifelong career service is being replaced with lifelong learning; internal promotions are being superseded by highly mobile individuals who sell their skills in the workplace.

With the reduction in the workforces of such giants as IBM and General Motors, it appears that the future will bring smaller "big" companies. Indeed, companies are remaking themselves in the image of their smaller, leaner competitors. Not only is the structure of the economy driving companies to downsize, but the realities of today's business world are also precipitating such reductions. In a world in which rapid change requires that businesses be flexible and highly adaptable, huge companies are at a distinct disadvantage.

In the past, large companies became so diversified that they had trouble following through with a single quality product line. Related to this, huge companies developed corporate structures that contained administrative and managerial levels that had to be traversed in order to get anything going. Thus, downsizing became essential. It meant that companies began to remake themselves in the image of smaller companies by decentralizing—placing power and control in the hands of units and departments.

Implications for Job Placement The most obvious may be the loss of jobs for people with disabilities who are actually employed, although downsizing may have little direct impact on overall employment given the fact that many people with disabilities remain unemployed. However, competition for existing jobs will be keener. More competition for available jobs does not mean that people with disabilities will be left out, but it does mean that job placement personnel must revise their job placement strategies, making them more in line with the marketing approach espoused in this book.

Downsizing may also affect job placement agencies in that they may be forced to imitate businesses by themselves downsizing. With the decreasing availability of public dollars, job placement agencies need to decentralize in order to respond more quickly and flexibly to environmental changes. Abolishing layers of mid-management personnel who have become part of programs over the years (e.g., service coordinators) is one way in which agencies may respond to new economic realities. This concept is discussed in more detail later in this section.

Employee Empowerment As companies change, employees are demanding more say, having more input into organizational processes, and demanding a fair share of company profits. In fact, in Rosenbluth and Peters (1992), it is argued that service agencies need to concentrate more on employees than on customers. In other words, without satisfied and empowered employees, customer satisfaction is difficult to achieve. Therefore, businesses are satisfying employees by providing a greater range of services at the workplace, by investing in employee retraining through various educational incentives, and by shifting to team approaches to encourage autonomy and share power.

Implications for Job Placement Employee empowerment is more important for human services and job placement agencies than for other professional service organizations for the simple reason that, when employees are regarded as being powerless or as having no voice, it is difficult for them to give voice to and to share power with jobseekers with disabilities.

Similarly, empowered employees are innovative ones. Employees who are directly involved in evaluating their own performance, in establishing their own performance goals, and in developing collaborative and creative opportunities for achieving personal and group goals are those who have a greater commitment to their agency and its positive change. This factor has been demonstrated repeatedly in business literature (see Rosenbluth & Peters, 1992). The payback to the agency is obvious: these employees are more willing to engage in problem-solving activities, to tackle difficult assignments, and to work to change and shape organizations for the future.

Building a Sense of Community at the Workplace   The Frederick Taylor Scientific Management Approach relied on steep vertical structures that clearly defined who reported to whom with regard to the internal hierarchy of command (Hummel, 1982). Each person had a clearly defined place on the corporate ladder, and the road to the top in terms of career mobility and job opportunities probably looked overwhelming for a worker situated at the bottom. This was how one could describe the corporation in newly industrialized America. As a result of complex changes and shifts in management styles and workplace organizations, however, this strict hierarchical structure is being replaced with flatter organizational infrastructures that focus more on particular tasks and the teams that are responsible for accomplishing them.

As a parallel process to the development of this flatter, more collaborative workplace structure, management theorists are placing increasing emphasis on workplace culture—the quality of life at work and its relationship to a person's overall quality of life. Not surprisingly, better workplaces—more accommodating and flexible atmospheres characterized by more individualistic and empowering cultures—produce more satisfied workers who performed better. These flatter hierarchies are evidenced by an emphasis on team approaches to get jobs done. These teams represent more than merely problem-solving entities; they represent attempts to build community at the workplace so that it is responsive to unique individual as well as group needs. Incorporating childcare centers at workplaces and allowing for family leave, peer review, mentoring programs, and health promotion activities are all trends shaping workplace communities.

Implications for Job Placement   Building a sense of community at the workplace, focusing on the quality of life at work, and concern regarding job satisfaction are trends that have come late to the job placement field. It may be that traditional human services work was seen as a reward in itself. This attitude may have promoted the idea that job placement agencies did not have to respond to the human element, that it was unnecessary to be concerned with the quality of life at work for employees.

An ironic example of how establishing a sense of community at the workplace has been ignored by job placement agencies is evidenced by a current program trend. There has been much attention given in recent literature regarding the idea of facilitating natural supports in the workplace by enhancing and/or maximizing existing supports for workers with disabilities so that the quality of work life is improved as they become more integrated into the workplace culture. This focus on enhancing existing supports through such means as mentoring programs and worksite training does not flow from what is routinely provided in job placement agencies and other human services organizations, but rather from what is typically provided in private sector businesses. In fact, Patterson and Fabian (1992) point out the inadequate provisions of workplace mentoring for personnel in a variety of rehabilitation programs. Thus, job placement professionals are in the ironic position of developing and promoting a concept that has been neglected in their own workplaces. Indeed, do agencies provide real chances for employees to develop skills and networking opportunities through mentoring programs, exposure to peers, or additional skills training? How difficult is it to persuade job placement personnel to help workers with disabilities in building a community of support in the workplace when they do not have a model in their own places of work?

"Smaller Is Better"   Osbourne and Gaebler (1992) call the trend toward smaller organizations and smaller units within larger organizations "chunking and hiving." That is, successful businesses are breaking large departments into smaller work units that can: 1) respond more quickly to environmental changes, 2) operate as entrepreneurial units within the larger context, and 3) tend to have a flat structure focused on performance and outcomes rather than on inputs and processes. This type of focus in turn allows larger corporations to streamline response time, thereby enabling them to compete with smaller businesses.

Implications for Job Placement   Certainly, for those large agencies that offer a variety of different programs, chunking and hiving allows smaller departmental units to more adequately respond to changes in the environment.

Chunking and hiving was exemplified by a large agency in the Washington, D.C., area that has an annual budget of about $3 million and provides a variety of services: psychiatric day treatment, vocational day programming and planning, residential services, outpatient mental health services, and psychosocial rehabilitation. Operating as a large unit, decisions once were difficult and several levels of management staff were involved in day-to-day decision making. By chunking programs and giving managers of individual units autonomous control regarding budgetary and programmatic decisions, the agency began to innovate more rapidly. For example, the vocational day planning program received a federal grant to develop innovative job placement strategies for young adults with dual disabilities. Additionally, the outpatient mental health services department opened up satellite offices in response to the demand for its service specialization. These programs subsequently succeeded or failed based on their own merits. Consequently, such autonomous freedom encouraged real change throughout the agency.

Focusing on Accountability and Performance   The private sector understands well the concepts of accountability and performance. After all, profits drive businesses, and profits are the measure of performance and subsequent accountability. Indeed, if customers are not satisfied or products are shoddy, profits will eventually decrease. In fact, there is a direct relationship between customer satisfaction and measures of performance. The fact that businesses now focus on performance measures is an attempt to share accountability across the organizational structure. This is also part of the "smaller is better" thinking, whereby a specific unit or team achieves its goals and receives recognition without focusing attention solely on top management personnel.

Implications for Job Placement   For the public sector, determining accountability and performance measures is more difficult. How do you measure the success of job placement agencies? More agencies are moving toward quantifying or specifying performance measures as the growing demand by consumers, funding agencies, parents, and advocacy organizations dictates. For example, if the purpose of a work adjustment training program is to increase the number of jobs available to participants, how will you measure that such a goal is accomplished? In the past, the measure tended to be the number of individuals participating in work adjustment training. However, this can also be a measure of failure; if many of the participants are not achieving the necessary skills, they are not getting competitive jobs. Therefore, a better measure of success would be to determine the number of individuals who actually obtain competitive jobs after participating in a work adjustment training program. A further measure may be how long these individuals remain competitively employed. Although it can be argued that various conditions and circumstances can affect these measures, it is nevertheless a move toward results-oriented measurement. The important point here is to start thinking in terms of performance and accountability. How does each job placement agency make a difference? How can you assess the difference they are making?

Mobile Workforces Just as the myth of long-term job security is being challenged by the recent downsizing of corporate giants, so too is the idea of lifelong employment using fairly specialized skills being challenged by the advent of the mobile workforce. Businesses place high priority on continually improving employees' skills in response to market demands. More emphasis is being placed on workers with generic skills—abilities to problem solve, to think creatively, and to generalize skills across jobs. Workers are now expected to develop and to continue to develop skills that are transferable across working environments. Consequently, workers are able to use skills throughout a highly mobile career path, changing jobs and even careers in order to find more challenging or better work assignments and benefits.

Implications for Job Placement How can individuals with disabilities, particularly those with significant disabilities, keep pace with the constant necessity of updating skills? Obviously, one way is through employer partnerships. Through such partnerships, job placement agencies can keep abreast of changes in expected worker skills and move accordingly to meet demands. It may well be that an individual cannot perform the skills required for a particular job. However, this individual could serve as part of a team, providing integral assistance and support needed to maintain pace or to ensure quality performance.

Tina, a woman with mental retardation, was placed in a biotechnology corporation working in a stressful environment with scientists and other professionals. A factor in that environment was simply ensuring that relevant research articles were copied and disseminated to appropriate staff in a timely fashion. Tina worked directly with one of the administrators on a team that identified articles for copying and checked off on a written form who was to get them. Thus, Tina's daily job was simply to ensure that the appropriate people got the right articles.

For people with disabilities, this emphasis on a highly skilled workforce does not signal the end of employment. It does, however, mean that job placement professionals need to think beyond the stereotypical jobs into which people with significant disabilities are frequently placed. This will in turn require a greater investment of time for problem solving at the workplace than may have been demonstrated previously.

Investment in the Future Through Training and Lifelong Learning Employers are demanding a more skilled workforce, and they are providing the types of long- and short-term investments in their workers that will enable them to develop skills necessary in this regard. For instance, they are challenging public schools to redefine their goals and outcomes to ensure that students who graduate acquire basic skills in reading and math. Alternatively, they are making huge investments in on-the-job training that are believed to be necessary in order to make up for the failure of public school education (Fabian & Luecking, 1991).

Training is essential in order to keep up with rapidly changing technological demands in the workplace. For whatever reason, not only are employers investing in employee training at an unprecedented rate, but employees are investing in their own learning as well. The number of adults enrolling in continuing education and training programs has been steadily growing through the 1980s and 1990s. Indeed, people are investing in their own futures.

Implications for Job Placement Job placement agencies, like adult education programs, present opportunities for lifelong growth and development. These agencies thus need to think creatively about the ways in which they deliver services to people with disabilities and to create opportunities for persons, once employed, to take part in various programs to receive skill upgrading or assistance with new technology.

Sponsoring career development workshops or guest speaker seminars at local agencies is one way to ensure that persons with disabilities have access to new labor markets and job opportunities throughout the lifespan. Similarly, sponsoring seminars on the ADA or reasonable accommodations is a way in which the lifelong learning needs of people with disabilities can be met. Working with the staffs of local politicians is a good way to get access to appropriate speakers for these events.

Another important aspect of lifelong learning is ensuring that local community colleges are providing opportunities for citizens with disabilities to enroll in courses and that those courses are widely and appropriately disseminated. You can probably identify many more appropriate methods of involving your agency and consumers in lifelong learning experiences.

Recommendations for the Future

Families, professionals, consumers, teachers, and administrators must move forward and devise creative new programs that address current conditions and that are responsive to existing challenges. The following are several recommendations in this regard.

Empowering Consumers Although this idea is certainly not new, the feeling persists that it continues to be more a slogan than a reality. As long as programs for people with disabilities continue to be run by and for professionals, empowerment will remain more a catchy phrase than a commitment to action.

Although special education programs mandate multidisciplinary planning focused on individual needs, it is still a system that keeps students and parents removed from the planning process. Indeed, this process remains in the hands of school professionals rather than with the students, parents, and advocates who are ultimately forced to live with school-based planning for the rest of their lives. The fact that the recent legislative movement toward consumer and student empowerment has forced a political showdown between schools, teacher unions, and parents highlights the chasm that exists between the schools that educate students and the parents who support them.

Because students in transition programs frequently attend schools that are far from their home neighborhoods, the ability of parents to provide much of the planning and support for these students is hindered. Moreover, parents generally are not involved in the transition process and do not receive the types of training that will enable them to assist their children in acquiring employment opportunities as they exit school and enter adulthood.

Osbourne and Gaebler (1992) point out that the only way to empower people receiving various services is to shift those services so that they are customer driven (i.e., when resources and money are placed in the hands of the consumers and choices are left up to them). Although we are not yet at this point in either job placement or special education, empowering consumers is a critical means of validating services and of setting a standard of accountability for the people who use them. This empowerment can be accomplished: 1) by ensuring that consumers and their advocates are aware of alternatives, 2) by having consumers and their advocates in leading positions of power in organizations, 3) by having boards composed of consumers and advocates who have a clear voice and who demand accountability for programs, and 4) by having clearly articulated mission statements so that consumers can assess the worth and worthiness of programs.

Thinking and Acting Contextually   Traditional thinking in job placement has generally refused to look at the larger picture, becoming so invested in one particular type of program or specialized group of services that the whole becomes vague and disappears. However, job placement agencies, as well as special education programs and other types of related human services, need to explore their services as part of the entire economic, social, and political fabrics of their communities and states. This is contextual thinking.

For the individual consumer, contextual thinking involves the consideration of many factors, not simply his or her disability. For example, family factors, social factors, and cultural and gender concerns all shape that person's identity and will shape his or her future as well. Developing a service plan based on one's disability is inadequate and even unethical. On a programmatic level, contextual thinking entails determining what is already available in the community and subsequently developing something that is necessary but not yet available (i.e., self-advocacy training for consumers, specialized training for parents, and/or disability awareness training for area employers). Organizationally, contextual thinking involves being aware of the economic and social forces in the community and subsequently discovering how your agency can and does actively shape those forces. For example, if jobs become scarce in the local labor market, look into creating enterprise zones in partnership with other public and private organizations, developing unique products or services to sell, or rebuilding existing programs.

Organizational contextual thinking is exemplified by the actions of the executive director of a state rehabilitation center in a small city in Pennsylvania. This center is a huge facility, occupying more than 13 acres. It provides standard job placement services, including vocational and work adjustment training and job development. However, because the state was reducing funding of its various programs and it was operating in an area where unemployment was about 13%, the center had to develop a meaningful program for residents with disabilities that also contributed to the entire community. The director thus turned the center into a continuing education facility for job placement professionals, educators, and industrial users. He installed satellite technology and the center began providing community employment not only for participants, but for the larger metropolitan area as well.

Contextual thinking is synergistic; it affects the program, the consumers, the marketplace, and the larger community. It ideally takes advantage of existing opportunities or creates new ones.

Investing in Community   Too often, job placement agencies remain on the fringes of the community. Refusing to see themselves contextually as part of the overall community life, their insular isolationist stance encourages the myth that both they and the people they serve are somehow different and must therefore be treated differently.

Community awareness requires many programs and personnel to see themselves and their agencies as integral parts of the community. It entails that staff and consumers attend community events, not simply because such attendance is a good way to promote programs and meet employers (although these are good reasons), but because agencies may well represent a significant proportion of revenue for the community in terms of annual budgets and numbers of people employed. For example, consider a rehabilitation center in a small rural town with a $2 million budget and more than 50 local employees. The entire community has a stake in the program continuing to grow, and the program has a stake in investing its resources and time in commitment to the community in order for it to remain a viable business force.

Building networks and investing in communities need to be seen not simply as a means of achieving agencies' agendas, but as a means of incorporating agencies and empowering them in the communities in which they exist. This in turn requires that agencies actively demonstrate investment in the community, for example, by participating as a "giver" in local fund raising events. As was stated previously, TransCen once had its entire staff function as phone bank volunteers for a local public television station during its fund drive. Volunteering at children's events or at hospices with older persons, or supporting a local baseball team—these activities are tangible evidence of investment in the community.

Anticipating the Future   One dramatic trend in health care is a renewed emphasis on primary prevention, which makes practical and particularly fiscal sense. If you spend money on preventing diseases and disabilities through immunization or anti-smoking and safe sex campaigns, then you save money in the long run.

Unfortunately, most job placement professionals probably would not view their services or programs in terms of prevention. After all, the field of job placement deals with disabilities after they have become functional impairments. However, it should be concerned with prevention at least in terms of mitigating lifelong disability, dependency, or secondary problems such as substance abuse. By viewing job placement in this way, it becomes easier to plan strategically for the best use of dollars and resources. Otherwise, problems are not identified until they occur, and job placement professionals are left to react to rather than prevent them.

Consider the phenomenon of dual diagnosis—diagnosing co-existing mental health and substance abuse disorders. The problem of young adults with serious mental illnesses abusing substances was identified in research literature of the 1970s and 1980s. At that point, prevention programs aimed at increasing drug awareness training in psychosocial rehabilitation programs, cross-training substance abuse and mental health counselors to recognize symptoms and to share resources, and identifying systemic barriers to treating co-existing problems would have helped prevent the crisis that exists today. Instead, we have millions of cases of people with dual diagnoses, staff with no training in recognizing symptoms, system barriers to treatment, and duplication of services. Anticipatory thinking may not have forestalled this epidemic altogether, but it certainly would have mitigated its impact.

Similarly, although the needs of special education students who age out of the school system have been in evidence for well over a decade, only recently have attempts been made to build the types of bridges that form the basis for successful transitions. Even now, problems arise for these youth because they have no reasonable means of actually implementing transition plans due either to lack of adult services, uninformed parents, or lack of follow through. At this point, few communities utilize anticipatory thinking in terms of allocating resources for training parents, developing community support for implementing transition plans, or bringing entire communities together in solving the dilemma of inadequate adult services. One tragic result of the lack of anticipatory thinking is the plight of individuals with significant mental illnesses living on the streets.

Anticipatory thinking often requires contextual thinking; investing in the community; and empowering consumers, parents, and staff members. The social problems discussed above are not easily solved. Unfortunately, responses to date, which can be characterized as too little too late, have only served to exacerbate these problems. Indeed, it is true that an ounce of prevention would have been worth a pound of cure.

Why Make Changes for the Future?

The first reason to make changes for the future is that the realities of federal budget deficits and citizens' demands for reducing the escalating deficit mean that federal dollars allocated to the human services will ultimately be reduced. They can't be replaced with state dollars because they are already used to finance community services such as the police, teachers, and basic health care. As these funds become more scarce, opportunities for running human services programs will be in jeopardy, particularly if legislators can no longer be persuaded that such programs are indeed effective.

A second future reality is that consumers are becoming increasingly vocal in their demands for control over the service system. Job placement as well as other human services professions obviously have an interest in controlling both the acquisition and allocation of funds for services. However, the future looks as if extensive professional control will not be possible, as consumers and their advocates are waging a battle to gain control of service systems. Through proposed voucher systems and other service innovations, they will begin to at least help determine who gets funding. Empowering consumers as partners now means that the future will not be characterized as conflictual, but as collaborative.

Third, businesses and the business climate are changing. As these potential partners face increasing competition and challenge, they are going to look less favorably on philanthropic endeavors and more favorably on mutual return as a basis for partnerships.

CONCLUSION

Papers and books are filled with the language of "new paradigms." Osbourne and Gaebler (1992) describe paradigms as sets of assumptions that are shared by a number of people regarding the ways in which things work. Thus, new paradigms involve changing these sets of assumptions, thereby challenging the beliefs and even values of earlier models. Described in this way, it becomes apparent that changing a system—in this case, the system of job placement services—is not easy. Complicating this task is the fact that modern American society seems confused regarding its direction and growth. It is indeed apparent that there are many interrelated problems and issues that are not easily solvable.

Certainly, the challenges to job placement discussed in this book are less serious than some of those faced by American institutions such as the public schools, criminal justice, or health care systems. However, it is critical to imagine the future of job placement as part of an overlying though changing societal paradigm. Partnerships are about taking advantage of change and taking mutual responsibility for shared investments and outcomes. Therefore, job placement agencies must consider the types of changes that will create opportunities to build such partnerships.

REFERENCES

Fabian, E.S., & Luecking, R.G. (1991). Doing it the company way: Using internal company supports in the workplace. *Journal of Applied Rehabilitation Counseling, 22,* 32–36.

Hummel, R.P. (1982). *The bureaucratic experience.* New York: St. Martin's Press.

Lewin, K. (1951). *Field theory in sound science.* New York: Harper & Row.

Osbourne, D., & Gaebler, T. (1992). *Reinventing government.* New York: Plume.

Patterson, J., & Fabian, E. (1992). Mentoring and other career enhancement relationships for women in rehabilitation. *Journal of Rehabilitation Administration, 36,* 131–144.

Rosenbluth, H.F., & Peters, D.M. (1992). *The customer comes second.* New York: William Morrow and Company.

Appendix

A FOCUS GROUP STUDY

One way to improve services and to determine what local employers demand is through focus groups. TransCen collaborated with Marriott Corporation in organizing a focus group study to solicit the opinions of job placement personnel and local employers regarding employment for people with disabilities.

The focus group sessions made use of Marriott's Decision Center, a high-tech room containing a network of 15 personal computers. These individual workstations allowed each respondent anonymity in responding to focus group questions, and the network enhanced brainstorming because the participants were able to view the responses of one another at their individual stations.

METHODOLOGY

This exploratory study utilized an open-ended focus group methodology. Representatives of both job placement personnel and employers were invited to attend separate 2-hour focus group sessions at Marriott's Corporate Headquarters in Bethesda, Maryland. Job placement personnel were invited from each of the vocational rehabilitation programs in Montgomery County, Maryland. Similarly, employers were culled by sending invitations to 20 local employers in the Washington, D.C., area who work with job placement agencies.

The employer group consisted of 12 individuals, eight representing private industries ranging from a small restaurant to a multi national conglomerate, and four representing large government agencies such as the National Institutes of Health. The job placement personnel group comprised 11 individuals who were directly involved in the job placement process.

Responses from the focus groups were recorded using computer interactive software that allowed each participant to respond individually at his or her workstation while simultaneously viewing the anonymous responses of others. This technology is described in business journals as potentially expediting corporate problem solving and improving worker productivity (Kirkpatrick, 1992). Indeed, the interactive linking function encourages responsiveness because it guarantees anonymity and allows for individual response time.

Table A.1. Barriers to employment for people with disabilities

Job placement personnel	Average rating		Employers	Average rating
1. Negative employer attitudes	4.36	1.	Employer's fears	4.33
2. The recession	4.27	2.	Employer's prejudices	4.33
3. Poor job market	4.27	3.	Employer's ignorance of	4.33
4. People's misconceptions	4.27		disabilities	
5. Employer's fears	4.20	4.	Downsizing of organizations	4.22
6. Competition	4.09	5.	No experience working with	4.11
7. Lack of understanding	4.00		people with disabilities	
8. Lack of entry-level positions	4.00	6.	Entrenched misconceptions	4.11
9. General stigma	4.00	7.	Takes too much time and effort to	4.11
10. High demand for generic worker skills that people with disabilities lack	4.00		train	
		8.	No corporate-wide acceptance	4.11
		9.	Lack of training	4.11
11. Doubts about workers with disabilities	3.91	10.	Failure of top executives to set standards	4.00
12. Oversized caseloads	3.91	11.	Accessibility to facilities limited	4.00
13. Failure of employers to recognize potential	3.91	12.	Supervisors aren't trained	3.89
		13.	No exposure to people with disabilities	3.89
14. Fear of people who "look funny"	3.91			
15. Inflexible job market	3.90	14.	Competition	3.89
16. Transportation limitations	3.82	15.	Attitudes of supervisors	3.78
17. Stereotyping people with disabilities into certain jobs	3.82	16.	Few job openings	3.78
		17.	Concern about accommodations	3.78
18. Poor preparation of students with disabilities	3.82	18.	Job placement personnel do not understand climate of work environment	3.78
19. Lack of marketable job skills	3.73			
20. Lack of business involvement	3.73	19.	Better qualified applicants than people with disabilities	3.67
21. Lack of comprehensive services	3.67			
22. Financial disincentives	3.64	20.	Failure to restructure jobs	3.67
23. Lack of time for job placement	3.64	21.	Fear of costs involved	3.67
24. Lack of employer willingness to accommodate	3.64	22.	Poor follow-up services	3.56
		23.	Fear of unreasonable concessions to be made	3.56
25. Difficulty in facilitating job opportunities	3.64	24.	Lack of interviewing skills among applicants	3.56
		25.	Company policies not flexible	3.44

Each group—job placement personnel and employers—responded to three questions:

1. What are the barriers to employment for people with disabilities?
2. What characterizes agencies, businesses, and professionals as good partners?
3. What would facilitate more successful job placements for people with disabilities?

Each group member was allowed to generate multiple responses to each question. In fact, job placement personnel generated over 100 responses to the question regarding barriers to placement.

After group response periods were terminated—generally after 15 minutes—the network system displayed the entire group's responses for each participant to rate. Therefore, the final results of the focus groups included not only each individual response items, but also average group ratings of each response. Individual ratings were scaled 1–5, 5 indicating the greatest level of agreement.

Table A.2. Characteristics of good partners

Job placement personnel	Average rating		Employers	Average rating
1. Flexibility	4.73	1.	Provide follow up	4.67
2. Creativity	4.73	2.	Understand needs of supervisors	4.67
3. Willing to accommodate	4.64	3.	Understand job requirements	4.56
4. Company culture that encourages diversity	4.64	4.	Concerned with making good job matches	4.56
5. Open to communication	4.55	5.	Know applicant's abilities	4.56
6. Frank about reservations	4.55	6.	Show up quickly when concerns are presented	4.44
7. Willing to take risks	4.55			
8. Ask questions	4.45	7.	Knowledgeable about business needs	4.44
9. Receptive	4.45			
10. Previous success with employees with disabilities	4.45	8.	Have ability to match skills with job needs	4.44
11. Maintain lines of communication	4.36	9.	Learn everything about jobs in which applicants are placed	4.44
12. Willing to make changes	4.36			
13. Willing to allow for training time	4.36	10.	Can identify applicants for many positions	4.38
14. Practice of nondiscrimination in hiring	4.36	11.	Assist in initial job training	4.33
		12.	Visit the facility	4.33
15. Accessibility to transportation	4.27	13.	Develop relationships	4.33
16. Open minded	4.27	14.	Look at workplace environment	4.33
17. Progressive	4.27	15.	Assist in problem solving	4.33
18. Preparation of students with disabilities	3.82	16.	Specific about client skills	4.33
19. Purposeful desire to hire people with disabilities	4.18	17.	Continue to follow progress after placement is made	4.33
20. Willing to learn about people with disabilities	4.18	18.	Understand work environment	4.22
		19.	Very positive attitudes even when there are problems	4.22
21. Sensitive and caring	4.09			
22. Allow time for additional supervision	4.09	20.	Follow up on performance of individuals placed	4.22
23. Willing to make accommodations "beyond the law"	4.09	21.	Work closely with manager when placement is not a success	4.22
24. Not afraid of people with disabilities	4.09	22.	Provide training to supervisors and co-workers	4.22
25. Previous experience with people with disabilities	4.00	23.	Willing to establish long-term relationships	4.22
		24.	Readily available in emergencies	4.22
		25.	Able to identify job accommodations	4.11

RESULTS

In order to provide an opportunity to view the group's responses to each of the questions, the 25 most highly rated responses from each group to each question are presented in three tables. Twenty-five were selected in order to include only the most highly rated responses (i.e., those with a mean rating of 3.0 or better). Repetitive responses were not included.

Table A.1 identifies the top 25 responses to the question regarding barriers to employment for people with disabilities. An examination of the responses indicates that both employers and job placement professionals cited attitudes and prejudices as being the most significant barriers to job placement. However, other responses of job placement personnel were related to economic factors such as a lack of jobs, whereas many of the employer responses regarded factors like inadequate training and ignorance.

Table A.3. Things that facilitate more successful job placements for people with disabilities

Job placement personnel	Average rating	Employers	Average rating
1. More jobs	4.45	1. Management support	4.44
2. More time to do job placement	4.45	2. Strong corporate commitment	4.22
3. More time to network with employers	4.45	3. Strong role models for jobseekers	4.22
4. More flexible employers	4.40	4. Better understanding of people with disabilities	4.11
5. A better local economy	4.36	5. More qualified job applicants	4.00
6. More staff to reduce caseloads	4.36	6. Sensitivity training to all organizational levels	4.00
7. Well-trained job placement personnel	4.36	7. More direct training to corporate staff	4.00
8. Availability of entry-level jobs	4.27	8. Help in dealing with negative attitudes	4.00
9. Improvement in the national economy	4.20	9. Advisory committee of people with disabilities	4.00
10. Technology to assist in obtaining job information	4.18	10. Jobs that allow for job sharing	4.00
11. Increased public education	4.18	11. Referral agencies for qualified applicants	3.89
12. More aware job market	4.18	12. More education regarding disability	3.89
13. More qualified job placement personnel	4.09	13. Previous success	3.89
14. One person to specialize in job development and placement	4.09	14. More long-term support from agencies	3.89
15. Increased salaries for staff	4.09	15. Training on how to modify jobs	3.78
16. Coordination of job placement efforts between agencies	4.09	16. Ability to identify recruitment sources	3.78
17. School system that trains applicants	4.09	17. Follow-up services	3.78
18. Newsletters to disseminate success stories	4.09	18. Initial success stories that are organizationally disseminated	3.67
19. More job sharing	4.00	19. Incentives for hiring	3.67
20. More flexibility from funding agencies	4.00	20. More media coverage	3.67
21. Less red tape and paperwork	4.00	21. More governmental incentives to hire	3.56
22. More money	4.00	22. Referral agencies that are easy to work with	3.56
23. Education regarding disabilities	4.00	23. Job placement personnel more knowledgeable about business	3.56
24. Governmental support	4.00	24. Better understanding of accommodations	3.56
25. Centralized system for locating job leads	4.00	25. More employees with disabilities	3.44

The second question addressed the issue of what characterizes agencies, businesses, and professionals as good partners. In response to this question, most job placement personnel cited employers' personal characteristics such as flexibility, openness, and willingness. By contrast, employers cited service indicators such as follow up, responsiveness, and knowledge. Table A.2 outlines these data.

The third question asked what would facilitate job placements for people with disabilities. Responses from job placement personnel indicate that most were concerned with increasing internal resources such as money, time, and staff. However, employers espoused stronger internal supports for hiring as well as increased access to training and applicants. Responses to this question are presented in Table A.3.

REFERENCE

Kirkpatrick, D. (1992, March). Here come the payoffs from the PCs. *Fortune*, pp. 93–100.

INDEX

Page numbers followed by "t" or "f" indicate tables or figures, respectively.

Access problems, 11
Accessibility surveys, 106
Accommodations
  ADA requirement for, 26, 29, 111
  categories of, 70
  definition of, 69–70
  demonstration of, 102–103
  identifying potential needs for, 69–71
Accountability, 115–116
ADAAG Express, 106
African Americans
  unemployment rate for, 7, 8
  in workforce, 5
Americans with Disabilities Act (ADA) of
    1990, 3, 7–8, 21, 26
  education and training related to, 26, 103,
    112
Antidiscrimination legislation, 3, 7–8
Apologetic approach, 108–109
Asking for sale, 85–86
Assessment of jobseekers, 55–56, 66–71, 104
Assimilation, 13
Assistive technology, 3, 111
  assessing needs for, 104–105
Attitudes toward services, 31, 89

Barriers to communication, 57–58
Barriers to employment, 68–69
  asking potential employers about, 79
  focus group study of, 124t, 125
  see also Obstacles to employment
"Beg, place, and pray" approach, 3, 4, 18, 20,
  109
Bridges . . . from school to work program,
  45–48
  as catalyst for other programs, 46–47
  goals of, 45–46
  intern placements by occupational cate-
    gory in, 48t
  mutual benefits between TransCen and,
    48t–49t
  outcomes of, 48
  partnership for implementation of, 46
  structural model of, 47f
Business cards, 82

Business consultation, 99–110
  activities of, 101–106
    assessment, 104–105
    communication, 103–104
    conducting inventory, 105–106
    demonstration, 102–103
    facilitation, 103
    follow-up activities, 106
    instruction, 102
    preparation, 105
  attributes of outstanding consultants,
    106–107
  evolving roles for, 109
  by job placement professionals, 100–101
  keys to success in, 107–109
Business friendships, 84
Business letters, 84–85
Business organizations, 73–74
Business trends, 112–117
  building a sense of community at work-
    place, 114
  downsizing, 112–113
  employee empowerment, 113–114
  focus on accountability and performance,
    115–116
  growth, 9
  investment in future through training and
    lifelong learning, 116–117
  mobile workforces, 116
  "smaller is better," 115

Career goals, 61–62
Career management plan, 60
Child care, 5
"Chunking and hiving," 115
Civil Rights Act of 1964, 3, 7–8
Cold calling, 28, 85
Communication, 34–35, 56–57, 57t
  barriers to, 57–58
  for consultation, 103–104, 107
  cross-cultural skills for, 58t, 58–59
  listening biases and, 59–60
Community
  building sense of at workplace, 114
  investing in, 118–119

Community—*continued*
  local business, 82
Complaints, 89–90
Computer programs, 61
Conducting inventory, 105–106
Contacts for job leads
  building "credit" with, 85
  keeping track of, 85
  making new contacts, 83–84
  sources for, 73–74
  staying in touch with, 76
  turning into customers, 83
Contextual thinking, 118
"Corporate man," 112–113
Creativity, 92–93
Cross-cultural skills, 58t, 58–59
Cultural diversity, 4–5
Culturally competent job placement profes-
    sionals, 58t, 58–59
Culture(s)
  definition of, 58
  organizational, 12
  of service organizations, 12
  understanding and valuing, 58
  value of inclusion and, 13
Customer satisfaction, 4, 19–23, 87–96
  balancing needs of employers and
    consumers, 21–22
  client as customer, 20–21
  definition of, 88
  employer as customer, 19–20, 72
  principles of, 22–23
  service and, 87–88
  shaping customers' demand, 27–35
  strategies for facilitation of, 88–96
    customized services, 91–92
    factors that negatively affect customers'
      opinions, 92
    handling complaints, 89–90
    handling mistakes, 93
    the importance of having a sense of
      humor, 95
    learning from other fields, 94
    listening, 96
    outstanding performance, 94
    positive attitude, 89
    responding quickly, 90–91
    treating colleagues as customers, 95
Customer service orientation, 18–19, 50
Customers
  balancing needs of, 21–22
  definition of, 65
  effective communication with, 34–35,
    56–59, 57t–58t
  empowerment of, 117–118
  getting to know employer, 71–77
  getting to know jobseeker, 55–56, 66–71
  treating colleagues as, 95
  turning contacts into, 83
Customizing services, 91–92

Deming, W. E., 88–89
Dependent on-site care, 5
Developmental Disabilities Assistance and
    Bill of Rights Act of 1975, 7
Disability, definitions of, 8
Disability awareness training, 26, 103
Diversification, 113
Downsizing, 112–113

Economic recession, 4
Education and training, 6, 102
  on ADA and reasonable accommodations,
    26, 103, 112
  investment in future through, 116–117
Education for All Handicapped Children Act
    of 1975, 7
Employee assistance program, 39
Employee empowerment, 21, 113–114
Employers
  Bridges program with, 45–48
  consultation with, 99–110
    see also Business consultation
  as customers, 19–20
  delivering quality services to, 33–34
  effective communication with, 34–35
  getting to know, 71–77
  informing of available services, 80–86
  knowing products and services available
    to, 80–82
  marketing to, 79–86
  Marriott Corporation, 9, 20, 25, 40–45
  shaping awareness of products and
    services, 30t, 30–31
  Southland Corporation, 37–40
  viewed as adversaries or philanthropists,
    71
Empowerment, 21, 113–114, 117–118, 120
Environmental factors, 33, 111
Externalizing agency services, 28–33
  activities for, 31t
  focusing on quality outcomes, 30
  monitoring quality of services, 31–33, 32f
  rationale for, 28–30
  shaping public awareness of products and
    services, 30t, 30–31

Facilitating job placements, 126, 126t
Features-to-benefits approach, 25–26, 42, 73
  of *Bridges* program, 48t–49t
  with Marriott Corporation, 44t
  with Southland Corporation, 40, 40t–41t
Federal budget deficit, 120
Feedback from customers, 89–90
Flex time, 5
Focus group study, 123–126
  barriers to employment identified by, 124t
  characteristics of good partners identified
    by, 125t

methodology of, 123–124
results of, 125–126
things that facilitate job placements identified by, 126t
Follow-up activities, 106
Force field analysis, 111
Future
  of partnerships, 112–121
  reasons to make changes for, 120
  recommendations for, 117–121
    anticipating future, 119–120
    empowering consumers, 117–118
    investing in community, 118–119
    thinking and acting contextually, 118
  training as investment in, 116–117
  workplace of, 13–14

Getting to know employers, 71–77, 108
  analyzing all aspects of targeted jobs, 76
  becoming knowledgeable about business world, 72
  distinguishing between employer as individual vs. organization, 72–73
  knowing the decision-making process for hiring, 75–76
  knowing services and benefits for employers, 73
  letting employers know why you are contacting them, 74–75
  recognizing multiple contact sources and joining business organizations, 73–74
  staying in touch with contacts, 76
Getting to know jobseekers, 55–56, 66–71, 104
  being responsive, 71
  identifying barriers to employment, 68–69
  identifying potential accommodations, 69–71
  obtaining wide range of information about them, 66–68
  spending time with them, 66

"Hire the handicapped" campaigns, 3, 71, 99
Hiring process, 75–76
Holland Self Directed Search, 60
Human resources management issues, 4, 5
Humor, 95

Image, 108
Impression management, 33
  organizational capabilities, 34
  people, 33–34
  physical environment, 33
  procedures, 34
In Search of Excellence, 87
Incentives, 93
Inclusion, value of, 13

Income, 7
Individualized written rehabilitation plan (IWRP), 21
Information about jobseekers, 66–68
Informing employers of available services, 80–86
  adapting personal style, 85
  asking for sale, 85–86
  avoiding selling what is not wanted, 85
  building business friendships, 84
  building "credit" with business partners, 85
  conducting marketing presentations, 82–83
  considering business card a marketing tool, 82
  coordinating with colleagues, 85
  developing and using promotional materials, 82
  keeping track of contacts, 85
  knowing available services and programs, 81–82
  knowing what employers want and expect, 80–81
  making new contacts, 83–84
  marketing services rather than disabilities, 83
  studying local business community, 82
  turning contacts into customers, 83
  using business letters as public relations tool, 84–85
  using past partners as references, 83
Instruction, 102
Internally focused goals, 11–12, 28–29

Job analysis, 76
Job availability, 4
Job coaches, 41
Job redesign, 6
Job search structuring, 55–63
  becoming aware of listening biases, 59–60
  developing career management plan, 60
  developing cross-cultural skills, 58t, 58–59
  developing effective communication, 56–57, 57t
  developing vocational goals, 61–62
  getting to know jobseeker, 55–56, 66–71
  remembering that vocational choice is not related to disability, 62
  understanding barriers to communication, 57–58
  using hands-on methods to explore vocational options, 61
  using occupational resources, 61
  using standardized interest inventories, 60–61
Job sharing, 6
Job Training Partnership Act, 37, 44

Knowledge of business world, 72, 82
Knowledge of products and services, 80–82
Kuder Occupational Information Survey, 60

Labor demographics, 4, 6, 20
Labor market demands, 28
Learning
  lifelong, 116–117
  from other professional fields, 94
Letters, 84–85
Listening
  biases affecting, 59–60
  as marketing tool, 96
  skills for, 56–57, 57t
Long-term relationships, 18, 50

Marketing
  consistency in, 109
  dedication to marketing orientation,
    107–108
  developing and using promotional mate-
    rials for, 82
  internal, 33–34
  to potential employers, 79–86
    informing employers of available ser-
      vices, 80–86
    knowing products and services, 80
  referral, 109
  seminars for, 82–83
  of services rather than disabilities, 83, 108
  shaping customers' demand, 27–35
  use of business cards for, 82
Marriott Corporation, 9, 20, 25, 40–45,
    105–106
  critical questions related to program of, 44
    mutual return on investment, 45
    value of employees with disabilities, 44
  Decision Center of, 123
  development of Bridges program, 45–48
  focus group study with, 123–126
    methodology, 123–124
    results, 124t–126t, 125–126
  funding for program of, 44
  human resource problems of, 41–42
  job trainer employed by, 42–43
  mutual benefits between TransCen and,
    44t
  outcomes of pilot project of, 43–44
  partnership with, 42
  TransCen's investment in program of, 45
Marriott Foundation for People with Disabil-
    ities, 46, 79
Maryland Planning Council on Develop-
    mental Disabilities, 42, 44
Montgomery County Entry/Re-entry Employ-
    ment Task Force, 40
Mutuality, 12–13, 25–26
Myers Briggs Inventory, 60

Natural supports approach, 109
Networking, 73–74, 119

Obstacles to employment, 8–12
  business growth trends, 9
  disability undefined, 8
  internally focused goals of public service
    organizations, 11–12, 28–29
  Social Security system, 9–10
  Vocational Rehabilitation program, 10–11
Occupational Outlook Handbook, 61
On-site activities
  dependent care, 5
  of job placement agencies, 33
On-the-Job Training subsidies, 44
Organizational capabilities, 34
Organizational contextual thinking, 118
Organizational culture, 12
Outcomes, 4, 28
  of Bridges program, 48
  of Marriott Corporation project, 43–44
  qualitative vs. quantitative, 29, 30
  of Southland Corporation project, 39–40

Partnerships
  based on mutuality, 12–13, 25–26
  case studies of, 37–48
    Bridges program, 45–48
    Marriott Corporation, 40–45
    Southland Corporation, 37–40
  characteristics for effectiveness of, 17–19,
    19t, 49–50
    customer service orientation, 18–19, 50
    goals and objectives that benefit every-
      one, 18, 49
    long-term relationships, 18, 50
    service competence, 18, 50
    trust, 17, 49
  developed through consultation, 99–110
  focus group study of, 124, 125t, 126
  future of, 112–121
  marketing approach for development of,
    27–35, 35f
  weak, 25
Performance
  focus on, 115–116
  outstanding, 94
Personal style, 85
Peters, Tom, 87, 89, 92–94
Power Shift, 88
Prevention programs, 119
Problem solving, 89–90, 93, 107
Procedural delays, 34
Promotion, 13
Public awareness of products and services,
    30t–31t, 30–31, 32f
Public Law 66-236, see Vocational Rehabili-
    tation Act

Public Law 93-112, see Rehabilitation Act of 1973
Public Law 94-142, see Education for All Handicapped Children Act of 1975
Public Law 95-602, see Developmental Disabilities Assistance and Bill of Rights Act of 1975
Public Law 99-506, see Rehabilitation Act Amendments of 1986
Public Law 99-643, see Social Security Act
Public Law 101-336, see Americans with Disabilities Act of 1990
Public Law 102-569, see Rehabilitation Act Amendments of 1992
Public service organizations
  cultures of, 12
  internally focused goals of, 11–12

Quality of life, 5
Quality of services, 22–23
  customer satisfaction and, 87–96
  delivery of quality services, 33–34
  monitoring of, 31–33, 32f
Quality performance indicators, 35, 35f

Recruitment, 13
References for new contacts, 83
Referrals, 109
Rehabilitation Act of 1973, 3, 7, 10, 21
Rehabilitation Act Amendments of 1986, 7
Rehabilitation Act Amendments of 1992, 21
Resource books, 61
Responding quickly, 90–91
Responsiveness, 71
Retention, 13

Scheduling patterns for work, 5–6
Scientific Management Approach, 114
Seminars, 82–83
Sense of humor, 95
Service competence, 18, 50
Shaping customers' demand, 27–35
  communicating effectively with consumers and employers, 34–35
  delivering quality services, 33–34
  externalizing agency services, 28–33
  key actions for, 28
  rationale for, 27–28
Shaping public awareness, 30t–31t, 30–31
Skill Training Partnership initiative, 105
Small businesses, 9
"Smaller is better" thinking, 115
Social Security Act, 9
Social Security system, 9–10
  entitlement guidelines for, 9
  proposed remedies for problems of, 10

Southland Corporation, 37–40, 102, 105
  departure from traditional job placement roles in, 39
  early recruitment attempts of, 37–38
  emerging partnership with, 38–39
  employee assistance specialist for, 39, 105
  follow-up activities with, 106
  jobseekers with disabilities and, 38
  mutual benefits between TransCen and, 40, 40t–41t
  outcomes of pilot program of, 39–40
"Spin doctors," 30
Strong Vocational Interest Inventories, 60
Style, 85
Supported employment, 3, 7, 21, 41
Supports in workplace, 5–6

Targeted Jobs Tax Credit, 26, 44
Teamwork, 95
Telecommunication, 6, 111
Televideo Assessment, 104
"3-3-3 Assessment," 67
Transition from school to work, 3, 26, 37, 119–120
  case studies of, 37–48
    Bridges program, 45–48
    Marriott Corporation, 40–45
    Southland Corporation, 37–40
Trust, 17, 50

Unemployment rates, 3, 7

Vocational choices, 62
Vocational evaluation, 66, 104
Vocational goals, 61–62
Vocational interest assessment, 60–61
  hands-on methods for, 61
  using standardized inventories for, 60–61
Vocational Rehabilitation Act, 10
Vocational Rehabilitation program, 10–11
Volunteering, 119
Voucher system, 21

Workforce, 4–7
  cultural diversity of, 4–5
  implications for people with disabilities, 6–7
  mobility of, 116
  women in, 5
  workplace supports for, 5–6
Workforce 2000 study, 40
Workplace
  building sense of community at, 114
  of future, 13–14